FIRST WATER, TIGERS!

Member Certificate, lithographic print. VFD COLLECTION

FIRST WATER, TIGERS!

A History of the Victoria Fire Department

DAVE PARKER

Published by
SONO NIS PRESS
VICTORIA, BRITISH COLUMBIA, CANADA
1987

Canadian Cataloguing in Publication Data

Parker, Dave, 1945-
    First water, tigers!

    Bibliography: p.
    Includes index.
    ISBN 0-919203-75-2

    1. Victoria (B.C.). Fire Dept. - History.
2. Fire-departments - British Columbia -
Victoria - History.   3. Fire prevention -
British Columbia - Victoria - History.   I. Title.

TH9507.V53P37 1987   363.3′78′0971134   C87-091347-6

Financially assisted by the Government of British Columbia
through the British Columbia Heritage Trust,
and the Canada Council Block Grant Program.

Published by
SONO NIS PRESS
1745 Blanshard Street, Victoria, B.C., Canada V8W 2J8

Jacket photograph: Deluge set, Imperial Building Supply fire, 1970.
    PHOTOGRAPHER UNKNOWN, VFD COLLECTION

Designed by James Bennett and printed
and bound in Canada by
MORRISS PRINTING CO. LTD.
Victoria, British Columbia

CONTENTS

This book is for

the Firefighters of Victoria

with special thanks to
Linda, Alison, and my parents.

PREFACE AND ACKNOWLEDGEMENTS

A visit to Victoria's old Cormorant Street Fire Department Headquarters with my kindergarten class in the early 1950s was an important stage in researching and writing this book. It engendered an interest in firefighting that has persisted and grown over many years — not so many, however, as my friends would likely suggest. The apparatus, the danger, and the excitement — some firefighters would suggest sheer terror — characteristic of firefighting have always held an appeal for me. The evolution of the fire department and the city it served ran parallel in many respects, and the combination of both of these fascinating histories proved irresistible and provided me with a legitimate opportunity to indulge myself in both these interests.

Settling on a title for a book is an important part of the process, and inevitably, I received several suggestions, some of which might well have resulted in my decidedly premature demise if used. "Pump and Circumstance" was almost universally viewed with misgivings — I liked it. Others emulated earlier Sono Nis Press successes such as "The Pacific Pumpers" and "10,000 Gallons." These suggestions were likewise rejected out of hand. *First Water, Tigers!* was ultimately chosen. Found in an old fire company log, this expression is a real part of the story and evokes images of the early years when rivalry between the two volunteer fire departments, the Tigers and the Deluge, was intense, and to be the one to put "first water" on a fire was a fiercely contested honour.

There are a myriad of cliches which describe the production of a book as a team effort, and they are, by and large, quite accurate. It is quite humbling for an author to realize how many people are involved in his or her creation, but without this help, the book would likely not exist at all. Chief Mike Heppell has always been both generous and exceedingly helpful in the course of researching *First Water, Tigers!*, giving me access to the department's excellent Archives and answering my many questions concerning the operation of the department from the early 1960s, when he joined, to the present. He also spent considerable time reading the manuscript and eliminating misconceptions or errors.

The assistance I have received from the officers, firefighters, and administrative staff of the Victoria Fire Department has invariably been generous and unstinting. Deputy Chief Bert Wilkinson suggested useful contacts and told me quite a number of amusing and interesting stories of the department. Deputy Chief Pat Graham also made it possible for me to gain access to necessary information. Anne, Vickie, and Lynn tolerated my presence on numerous occasions and were always helpful. Lynn located plans for No. 5 Hall for me earlier when she worked in the City Engineering Department. Ray Barron and Bob Hamilton provided information on the apparatus and kept me up-to-date on what was happening. Firefighter Dave Noren, President of the Victoria Firefighters' Benefit Society, arranged for me to spend considerable time around No. 1 Hall, actually getting a feel for the normal operation of the department.

Brian Young and Pat Dunae, of the B.C. Provincial Archives, directed me to new information sources, some of which had just arrived in the collection. Peter Westoby was exceptionally helpful with photography, as was Ken Young of the Vancouver City Archives. Penny Seedhouse of the Victoria City Archives was always very helpful and more than willing to assist me in locating obscure information. My friend Frank DeGruchy, several of whose fine apparatus photos are included, is widely known as an apparatus expert. He spent considerable time going over both the manuscript and apparatus roster for accuracy. Irving Strickland, a well-known Victoria press photographer, has also made a major contribution to this book, both in the sense that many of the photos are his, and also in that his recollections have provided information for photo captions.

Victoria's press and commercial photographers have made a major contribution towards preserving the history of the city and the Victoria Fire Department. Whatever their original purposes in taking the photographs may have been, the record that has survived is magnificent and one which serves to bring the past alive. Wherever I have identified the photographer, I have included the name along with an indication as to which collection the print used was from. I regret that in some cases, I have not been able to determine the photographer whose work I have used although every effort was made to do so. Among those who have contributed are; Charles Gentile and Richard and Hannah Maynard in the last century, and William A. Boucher, Ken McAlister, W. Atkins, Irving Strickland, Bill Halkett, Jim Ryan, John McKay and Ian McKain in this. I am grateful to them for their talent and their effort.

There are numerous others who have made a contribution such as Lt.-Cmdr. Ted Clayards and Clive Prothero-Brooks. Hugh Lynn, in the course of interviews, gave me a good impression of the department during the era of horse-drawn apparatus as did Gray Russell, Percy Graves, and Joe Norman for the 1930s, and Mike Heppell, Brian Dallin and Frank Thoresen for the 1950s-1980s period. Bob Griffin, who is very knowlege-able in terms of local sawmilling, assisted me in keeping straight which mill was which. This was an important aspect of the story since fires at these mills on numerous occasions kept the department busy. Bob also identified a number of mill photos that proved awkward for me and located them on a map, an often difficult and confusing task. Jacques Noel Jacobsen, Jr., of Manor Publishing, Staten Island, N.Y., gave permission to use illustrations from his reprints of fire apparatus/equip-ment catalogues, and Victoria artist Brian McCandless has provided several line drawings of apparatus used by the department over the years.

My friends Peter Corley-Smith and Bob Turner, have been of immense assistance in proofreading several versions of the manuscript. They were also very supportive when it was necessary to buttress the morale of the author — they have frequently referred to their role as a "salvage operation." My wife Linda who has also been burdened with proofreading, has made many useful suggestions and has provided encouragement when it was badly needed. She has had to put up with a husband who lapses into a form of euphoria at the sight of a LaFrance pumper most would reserve for a Lamborghini. While as a baroque violinist she does not really share the fascination, she does tolerate it.

Dick Morriss and his crew at Sono Nis Press have made producing this book a pleasure. They are professionals and fine people, a rare combination. Pat Sloan, a volunteer firefighter herself, brought enthusiasm to the project. This did much to raise my spirits. I have promised her that someday soon I will learn to write without using colons — at last count the original manuscript had something like 8,412, possibly a record. This may be one reason why Smitty keeps threatening to "kill the Author." Glenda managed to stay awake while entering the manuscript into the computer, no mean feat when my writing is considered. Jim Bennett produced a book design that gave me everything I could have wanted and proved to be a pleasure to work with — especially once I promised not to add any more photos.

Victoria firefighters can look back on their accomplishments and the history of their department with pride. However, many aspects of their history are unknown to the people who have depended on the services of the department. I hope this book will bring to the public, and to the firefighters themselves, a perspective on the department which will reflect a long and important record of community service and dedication.

DAVE PARKER
August 1987, Victoria, British Columbia

FOREWORD

Michael E. Heppell, O.St.J., CD
Chief, Victoria Fire Department

This book represents a major contribution to the recorded history of the City of Victoria and more specifically to the men who served with distinction to keep their City and its citizens safe from the danger of fire.

From the earliest days of Fort Victoria when the greatest fire threat was found in the domestic preparation of food and provision of heat in small wooden buildings to the present day where bulk quantities of hazardous commodities such as gasoline and liquified petroleum gas are a part of our everyday life, the reader will experience the opportunity of following the evolution of Victoria and the corresponding development of its fire defences.

There is no doubt that the Victoria Fire Department did have a struggle for existence in its earlier years and that the intervening period has been punctuated all too frequently by detrimental cutbacks due to measures of economic restraint. Regardless, it is quite certain the result of these difficult experiences is the firm establishment of a sincere and lasting dedication toward fire safety along with a strong spirit of comradeship throughout the ranks of the Department, all of which is very accurately recorded in this fine history for which the author deserves particular credit.

I am indeed confident that those who have served with the Department will read this history with much pride for it is a most fitting tribute to them for a job well done.

Rodgers Manual Engine 1858   BRIAN McCANDLESS

"FIRE CALL!"

Early one July morning in 1867, just as many Victorians were arriving for a day's work, a dry goods clerk sweeping off the sidewalk in front of the store on Government Street noticed a wisp of smoke curling skyward from the rear of a wooden building across the street. He paused, leaning on his broom. Fascinated, he watched as what had only a few moments earlier been a hint of smoke, gradually became heavier. He noticed also that it was not coming from a chimney. Clearly, there was not any time to waste.

With his broom still clutched tightly in his hand, the clerk headed across the street to investigate. Others too, were becoming aware of the gathering smoke. The gap he entered between the two buildings was uncomfortably hot — there was no doubt now, it was a fire! — probably in the lean-to behind the building.

Tossing his broom aside, the clerk ran yelling "Fire! Fire!" to the Deluge Engine house a block away. Throwing open the door, he reached for the bell's rope and pulled hard. The bell rang out, instantly bringing all activity in town to a halt. Doctors left their patients, merchants their shops, and tradesmen dropped their tools. Volunteer firemen ran to their engines, grabbing helmets and tow ropes. Those who arrived first took their places on the engines' tow ropes, others, those of the two-wheeled hose carts. The Hook and Ladder Company also ran to their house and like the other firefighters, took the tow ropes — some to pull, others in the rear to assist with steering and braking so that those pulling would not be run down by their apparatus.

The two engine companies — the Tigers and the Deluge — ran as fast as they could along the dusty streets, each company hoping to be the first into action. Getting the "First Water" onto the fire was a great honour. Upon arrival at the fire, it was obvious that the Tiger engine — the first to respond — was too far from a cistern, the large underground tank from which they would have to pump water. The Deluge, arriving only slightly later, would have to operate in tandem with them, pumping water from the cistern to the Tigers' Button hand engine. The Tigers would then turn their hoses on the fire.

Being second was a hard blow for the Deluge company, but there was still some hope of winning glory, of disgracing the Tigers. If they could "wash" — overwhelm — the Tigers' engine and their ability to cope, the superiority of Deluge would be beyond dispute! Unfolding the brakes, the pumping handles, on their engine, up to twenty men at a time on each engine pumped madly — up to 120 strokes a minute! The pace was so frantic they changed men every two or three minutes as they tired.

Handles on both engines moved rapidly as the pumps sucked water from the tank and discharged it through the heavy leather hoses.

If the cistern ran dry, and there was the probability that it would soon do so, nothing more could be done to save the building. Fortunately for the owner, the building was insured. Bystanders noticed that there was a Fire Mark, the symbol of an insurance company and visible proof of coverage, mounted on the wall. If the worst happened and the structure could not be saved, it would be possible for the owner to rebuild.

The "lads" from the Union Hook and Ladder, the first formed of Victoria's volunteer fire companies, were ready if necessary to tear down the building, and possibly the structure next to it if the "fire demon" spread, out of control. They would have been forced to create a fire break, to deprive the fire of fuel. While the engine companies worked hard playing water onto the fire under the direction of the Chief Engineer, the Hook and Ladder men gained entry to the building and began moving stock across the road—something at least would be saved from the situation. Within a few minutes, the steady stream of water from the pumps controlled the fire and the men could catch their breath.

Luck was with them — the wind didn't blow — and the prompt response of the volunteers made it possible to prevent what might have become a catastrophe. Had this happened just over a decade before, nothing could have prevented disaster.

Chapter 1

A CLEAR AND INCREASING DANGER

Last evening the roof of Rudolph's Oyster Saloon, Waddington Street was discovered in a blaze. Had it occurred a day or so ago when the roofs were dry and the wind blew furiously, no one could guess at the result. When are we to have an effective fire department? This is a warning.

The British Colonist,
Victoria, Vancouver Island, June 1859

Fire! Controlled it can provide vital warmth, cook food, and process materials we need in almost every facet of our lives. But uncontrolled, it can destroy lives, structures, whole cities and forests. Well into the nineteenth century, even with the new technology of the industrial revolution thrown into the battle, it seemed impossible to prevent disaster when the "fire demon" went on the rampage. Large cities like New York, Chicago, Seattle, and later, San Francisco, were to feel its wrath. Any threat of fire was terrifying and steps had to be taken to combat it. Not everyone always appreciated these concerns, however.

The Hudson's Bay Company had established Fort Victoria on the southern tip of Vancouver Island as the headquarters of their maritime fur trade in 1843. The site chosen for the fort was on the eastern shore of a superb land-locked harbour and so provided an excellent facility for ships bringing furs from the northern coast. Victoria in the early spring of 1858 was a frontier fur-trade settlement with a population of scarcely 300 people and in contrast with larger centres, little if any thought was given to the danger of fire. The majority of citizens were connected with the Hudson's Bay Company and were bound by company discipline—they could be expected to exercise care. There had never been a fire in the fifteen years since the fort was built and people had become complacent. In any case, not many activities in the town involved the use of fire, so few worried.

This settlement was still the only town of consequence in what was at that time a vast wilderness. San Francisco, some 1,000 miles by sea to the south, was the nearest large city. Edgar Fawcett, who arrived in the town in 1858, recalled his impressions of the fort and the area surrounding its walls in his *Reminiscences of Old Victoria.*

The first thing that attracted our attention on coming into the harbour was the high palisade of the fort.... In the centre of the large gates were smaller ones. These small gates were opened every morning at seven o'clock on the ringing of the fort bell, which was suspended from a kind of belfrey in the centre of the yard.

Fire Marks, essentially tin badges, were mounted on structures as proof of insurance. This was especially useful in England where insurance companies paid firefighters to protect their clients' property. These marks still exist in the Victoria City Archives.

To the north were the stores and warehouses, and to the south, large barns; the residences were situated on the east side of the fort...Fort Street...was composed of boulders, which being round made rough riding, and so muddy, too! Try and imagine it. The sidewalk was of two inch boards, laid lengthwise, three boards wide...and ran up three or four blocks....The country around View and Fort Streets, up to Cook, was very swampy, and covered by willow and alder trees. In fact there was a small swamp or lake on View street, where there was good duck shooting in the winter.[1]

As will so often happen, however, this idyllic situation changed and with it, the danger of fire increased dramatically. Gold was discovered on the Fraser River in the spring of 1858, and word of the discovery spread far and wide: south to California, east to Canada and the Atlantic coast, and even to Europe and Australia. A gold rush resulted, which was similar to the one which took place in California almost a decade earlier in 1849.

Almost overnight, Victoria was transformed. The size of the population, both permanent and temporary, increased tremendously, and the whole character of the settlement changed. From a tiny village with a homogeneous population, it burst into a bustling city of several thousand people with varied backgrounds. Shiploads of people continued to appear from over the horizon as prospectors and businessmen arrived by the thousands. The town became very crowded indeed.

Everyone bound for the gold fields was required to pass through Victoria. James Douglas, the Governor, was concerned that the Americans would inundate the territory and then assume control as had happened earlier in Oregon. He insisted that all the miners were required to buy the necessary food, tools and licences, and only then could they arrange travel to the Fraser. This regulation benefited local businesses, including the Hudson's Bay Company, and encouraged many to try and get rich serving the miners rather than heading for the "diggings" themselves.

While in Victoria, all these people had to find a place to live or set up their businesses. The prospectors camped out in tents, most of which were little better than cloth stretched over poles and, with little clear land available, they had to set up wherever there was room. Consequently, the threat of a catastrophic fire was very real. The editor of the *Weekly Gazette*, appalled by the congestion, described the scene, graphically referring to it as the "Arab mode of existence."

Hundreds of these miniature dwellings are scattered through our suburbs, some choking up ravines with their numbers, others spread out on the broad plain that surrounds the city. Others still spring up on the shores of the bay remote from the town's centre.[2]

The transients cooked over open fires built close to their highly flammable tents, and this posed a very real danger. A fire, once started in the encampment, could spread quickly to the town itself probably wiping it out. The miners were far from being the only problem. Those who were to remain after the miners booked passage, the businessmen who provided goods or services to the more permanent residents, were also adding to the fire threat and they presented an even greater danger to the community.

[1] Edgar Fawcett, *Some Reminiscences of Old Victoria*. Toronto, William Briggs, 1912, p. 28.

[2] "Camp Life Around Victoria," *Weekly Gazette*, 10 July 1858, p. 2.

As the number of businesses and trades increased to serve the growing population, so too did the number of buildings necessary to house them: more than 250 buildings were constructed between June 12 and August 21, 1858.[3] Some of the businesses housed in these often ramshackle structures—restaurants, blacksmiths, tanneries and laundries—used fire in the normal course of their work, greatly increasing the danger of a catastrophic blaze in town. Despite this very real danger, people were free to do as they wished without regard to safety. Fire codes or any other regulations to ensure that fire was used carefully did not then exist.

Vancouver Island and mainland British Columbia were both British Crown Colonies at this time. The Governor, the Executive Council and the House of Assembly—the local government of the period—did nothing though they were permitted after August 1856 to enact such fire protection laws. The local population was indifferent to the danger, an attitude characterized by the politicians who would have to enact the laws making any efforts all but impossible. Even the community leaders simply did not care! Later, when looking back over these years, Dr. J. S. Helmcken, one of the politicians who was formerly a Hudson's Bay Company doctor, and therefore an influential member of the community, mentioned in his *Reminiscences* that "somehow we [as Members of the Assembly] could not comprehend and did not believe the change in Victoria to be permanent... legislation became irksome, and it was hard to get people together—they had better work to do."[4]

In the absence of any controls whatsoever there were numerous other problems which added to the fire hazard situation in Victoria. Gunpowder was stored in the fort in unsafe conditions and posed a serious potential danger if a fire were to spread. It was not stored at a safe distance from residential areas, and so it could prove extremely dangerous if it were to blow up. Surprisingly, the seemingly commonplace could prove a serious threat: stovepipes, even in buildings, let alone tents or shacks, were being put up with a total disregard for fire safety. They were placed hard up against wooden surfaces and some were not even properly assembled, with gaps being left between sections of pipe. Sparks could easily escape and land on tinder-dry wooden roofs.

This particular danger was recognized by the ever-vigilant press, the editor of the *Gazette* cautioning that "the expedient of a stovepipe hole rather than a chimney is an unsafe one and should not be resorted to by anyone regardful of his own interests or the public safety."[5] As early as January 1859, a Grand Jury report indicated an awareness of the problems, and made several recommendations to decrease the fire danger in general. But still no legislative action was taken by the government.

There was an additional hazard that compounded the unsafe conditions and would greatly speed the spread of fire: the plan of the town was becoming utterly chaotic. Tents, huts, lean-tos, and even more substantial buildings were being put up in locations that blocked or altered the course of existing streets. They were placed wherever their builder could find space. There were strident pleas by correspondents in the *Gazette* that the streets should be cut through, even if this did mean pulling down a few buildings.[6] Then, the letter writers suggested, if the town could be laid out in a grid pattern with wide streets, the spaces created would serve

[3] "Improvements in Victoria," *Weekly Gazette*, 21 August 1858, p. 2.

[4] J. S. Helmcken, *Reminiscences*, (ADD. MSS 505/A810), vol. 4, p. 12.

[5] "A Hint," *Weekly Gazette*, 3 July 1858, p. 2.

[6] "Destructive Fire," *British Colonist* (hereinafter referred to as the *Colonist*), 19 October 1859, p. 2.

Fort Victoria, viewed from the south side of the harbour. When this photo was taken in 1858, the city seems as peaceful as it is today.
PABC HP93855

Looking east from the Songhees reserve towards "downtown."   BCPM

Key to photographic sources

BCPM   British Columbia Provincial Museum
PABC   Provincial Archives of British Columbia
VCA   Vancouver City Archives
VFD   Victoria Fire Department

Sir James Douglas, looking decidedly ill at ease in his Vice-regal uniform, was a capable and respected Governor but tended to be somewhat autocratic.
PABC HP2656

Victoria in the 1860s resembled a typical "wild west" town. This photo, identified as Wharf Street, shows the false fronts, wooden sidewalks and verandahs that added to the charm of the city but also to the fire danger.   PABC 12178

Before long, brick buildings on Government Street imparted an air of sophistication and permanence to the city. A water cart is shown on the right in this 1860s view.   PABC 7893

as excellent firebreaks. The fire could not jump across the gaps even when a stiff wind was blowing and instead of spreading, it would be contained within the blocks where it originated. But there had to be other, equally fundamental changes to the buildings themselves.

Virtually all the buildings in town were constructed of wood which was both inexpensive and readily available. False fronts, wooden verandahs and sidewalks, as was then the fashion, connected the buildings giving Victoria the appearance of a typical "wild west" town. While useful for advertising the business concerned, the false fronts greatly increased the speed with which a fire could spread by providing a path from building to building.

Balloon-frame walls were another problem caused by construction methods of the period. Hollow from the foundation to the roof and lacking separators of any kind, such as floor joists, they did nothing whatever to slow the spread of fire. In fact, the space between the walls acted exactly like a chimney. To compound these problems, no attempt was made to regulate the size of buildings nor to separate hazardous businesses or trades from each other or from residential areas. There was no zoning. It was essentially the same problem as that posed by gunpowder storage.

Circumstances had combined to create a serious danger of fire and, to an increasing number of people in town, it seemed as though Victoria's destruction was both imminent and inevitable. The town had been extremely fortunate to this point, but would its luck hold?

A Time for Action

In the late spring of 1858, shortly after the onset of the gold rush, permanent residents petitioned Governor James Douglas for some form of fire protection. Foremost among those signing the document were local businessmen who had by this time made a substantial investment in their buildings and stock. While action regarding the enactment of legislation, at least initially, had been less than frantic, Douglas responded very quickly to the plea and ordered British Columbia's first fire apparatus from San Francisco. George Hossefross, a former San Francisco Chief Engineer, acted as the Governor's intermediary in California. Truett, Jones, and Arrington, the company from which the apparatus and equipment were purchased, incidentally, had a stake in keeping Victoria safe from fire. The company had recently begun construction of a wood-frame building on Wharf Street to house a Victoria branch of their business.

Two hand-operated pumpers, one used, and one newly-manufactured, were acquired for use in Victoria. Hossefross had been with San Francisco's Monumental Engine Company from 1851-1853, a fact which undoubtedly influenced the choice of the first engine. This machine, a Baltimore-built Rodgers type, had been part of an order of three engines purchased new for San Francisco in 1850. Hossefrosse would have been familiar with it, and it also had the virtue of being readily available. The indenture, or purchase agreement, indicated that the Hudson's Bay Company paid $1,600, and that the price included 500 feet of hose and a cart to carry it.[7]

[7] *Indenture*, (PABC Ms. F789/1).

The other engine, purchased new, was a second-class machine built by Hunneman and Company of Boston, an important manufacturer at that time. Listed in the purchase agreement as having a pump with a 6-inch cylinder with a 14-inch stroke, the engine was somewhat cryptically described as being "Carmine with a red stripe." In a period when fire engines were usually quite ornate, almost works of art in terms of their liveries, Victoria's little Hunneman seems to have been an economy model. The purchase price of $1,750 included a hose cart or "jumper." Fire engines seldom carried their own hose at this time.

A further $1,647 was spent on hose (1,014 feet of it to serve the Hunneman) and to clear up miscellaneous expenses relating to the purchase. Hose at this time was very different from the type in use today. It was made of cowhide joined by rivets, was extremely heavy, and required considerable care in handling. Both after use or while lying idle for some time, the leather had to be kept pliable by applications of neat's-foot oil, or a similar leather conditioner. Though this was at best a messy, time-consuming process, without it, the hose would stiffen and crack.

Hand-powered engines — "manuals" — including those purchased for Victoria, were the only type of fire engines in use in the 1850s. They were basically wooden 4-wheel carts equipped with a pump and towing ropes. The pump was operated by firemen alternately lifting and pushing down the "brakes" or pump handles at a high rate of speed. Engines were classed according to the position of the brakes: either end or side stroke. Double deckers, yet another class, had firemen manning the brakes both on the ground and standing on the engine. The engine's capacity was also part of its classification. Later sections of this book will explain the nature of fire-fighting technology and methods.

For a total of $5,020.47, Victoria, or more accurately, the Hudson's Bay Company, now had the basis of a fire department. Governor Douglas, to whom the invoice was issued, paid it from Hudson's Bay Company funds. This was reasonable since the Company was required to pay all expenses of this kind by virtue of the 1849 charter that granted the Company quasi-governmental powers over Vancouver Island and the mainland in exchange for the extension of the fur-trade monopoly. In order to retain these rights, the Company was required by the British Colonial Office to assume a number of "municipal" responsibilities. It was an unexpected expense, however, because when the Company had agreed to the terms of the Charter, the gold rush and its effects, which sharply escalated civic responsibilities, could not have been foreseen. Ironically, the gold rush finished off an already dwindling fur trade as settlement and the fur trade were incompatible. Meanwhile, another problem that had to be addressed was the water supply.

A reliable water supply was obviously a necessity. It was not only vital for drinking and cleaning purposes, but a fire department would be useless without it. It was a requirement that could not be easily satisfied. Douglas had been concerned about the water situation for some time and had made strenuous efforts towards providing an adequate source as early as 1850 when the population of the settlement was still very small. In a letter to his superior, Archibald Barclay, in December of that year, he wrote of his failure when attempting to drill for water — his workers had encountered the extremely hard rock that has plagued others drilling or excavating in Victoria ever since that time. The initial attempts were unsuccessful but, given the importance of the work he was not about to give up.

We therefore transferred our operations to the Valley of a winter rivulet about 400 yards distant, where we hope to find a sufficiency of fresh water . . . and when that object is accomplished, we shall if circumstances permit, make our further trials more immediately in the vicinity of the Fort, as in case of fires occurring about the premises that useful element cannot be too much at hand.[8]

Douglas was apparently not entirely successful in this effort, because eight years later, in 1858, Victorians were having to purchase their fresh water from two sources for domestic use; either from a spring owned by the Hudson's Bay Company, or a water cart that made deliveries to the door. In the latter case, the water was brought from the Sooke area in a tank-equipped schooner, and then transferred to the water carts at the Hudson's Bay Company wharf for distribution.

It was expensive and, needless to say, cumbersome. This system did work after a fashion when the population was small and there was almost no call for large amounts of water. It was obvious though, that there would be problems in the event of an emergency. Sea water from the harbour was almost as unsuitable for fire-fighting as it was for drinking as salt is highly corrosive and would damage both metal parts in the engines and the copper rivets in the leather hose. The water supply situation will be explored at greater length later.

The engines arrived on the steamer *Oregon* on July 28, 1858, and the first test took place in the compound of the fort that same day with water being drawn from a well. The *Gazette*, in an article published the following day, described the event.

The brakes were manned by individuals volunteering from the crowd drawn together to witness the throwing of the first water by a fire engine in our town, among whom we noticed several old San Francisco firemen. The machines are rather small, but sufficiently powerful to throw a full stream of water over any building in town with ease.

Now that he had received the apparatus, the Governor's next step was to create some sort of organization with which to fight fires, and not insignificantly, to care for the apparatus and equipment. Douglas placed the responsibility for the "fire department" in the hands of Police Commissioner Augustus F. Pemberton. Edward Coker, a Hudson's Bay Company blacksmith, was entrusted by Douglas with the care of the apparatus and equipment. This was a practical move, since Coker, by virtue of his trade, undoubtedly would have been carrying out repairs on them in any case and he was already employed by the owners of the engines.

When people became convinced of the necessity for action, things happened quickly in old Victoria. Within three days of the engines' arrival, Victorians held a public meeting to organize a fire department of their own. Their plan was simple: if a fire were to break out, those citizens

Victoria's little Hunneman manual pumper was new when purchased by the Hudson's Bay Company in 1858. Fire-fighters pumped using the handles on each side of the rig.

BRIAN McCANDLESS

[8] Hartwell Bowsfield, ed., *The Fort Victoria Letters: 1846-1851.* Winnipeg, Hudson's Bay Record Society, 1978, vol. XXXII, p. 39.

who had already informally organized themselves into two companies (Engine Co. No. 1 to crew the Hunneman, and Telegraph Co. No. 2, the Rodgers) were to run to the fort where the apparatus was stored. Then, presumably supervised by Pemberton, they were to put out the fire. Coker's role in all this was somewhat ambiguous despite the fact that he had been given the rather inflated title of Superintendent of Fire Engines.

This "department," however, was almost totally unstructured. Apart from the separation into the companies by the citizens themselves, and apart from Douglas' appointments at the top, there were no positions of authority at the company level which could be clearly identified. Americans in the community, who were familiar with such institutions at home, were undoubtedly responsible for an effort to organize a proper volunteer department in early August 1858, complete with constitution and bylaws for each company. In the United States, volunteer fire companies had been in operation since the eighteenth century and this had become the standard form of fire protection in many parts of North America.

In Victoria, this first effort towards creating a volunteer department failed, and nothing further was attempted at this time to create such an organization in Victoria. Gold fever had declined, and the vast majority of the Americans had left town, temporarily at least, apparently taking with them any enthusiasm for an organized department. Apathy resulting from a lack of fires may also have decreased the sense of urgency and, as a consequence, Victoria continued to depend on Coker and his unorganized volunteers for several months. The only obligation on citizens to respond to an alarm was self interest: if they did not take a hand to protect their own property, who would?

The necessity of having people clearly identified as being in charge at the company level soon became apparent to Douglas. In January 1859, a few months after the first abortive attempt to create a volunteer department, Edward Coker and C. S. Simpson were appointed chiefs or captains of the fire department by Douglas and were given the power to organize fire companies.

Lessons learned from the earlier efforts at organizing fire companies were ignored as apparently were the wishes of the citizens who were expected to provide the manpower. It was obvious from the fact that Douglas had appointed these people that new organization was not to be of the democratic American pattern, in which officers were elected by the members themselves. Nothing much had really changed and Pemberton likely still retained overall responsibility, perpetuating many of the problems.

The political situation at this time was sensitive; many people in the community were offended by the paternalistic attitude and methods of the government — the Hudson's Bay Company. *Colonist* editor Amor De Cosmos was a Nova Scotian by birth, and had seen the struggle there against the rule of an oligarchy, a privileged and therefore powerful group within the community. Another newspaperman, Joseph Howe, also a Nova Scotian, had become well known for his successful crusade against this situation in that region. De Cosmos saw himself as being very much in this same mould: he was crusading against privilege and for responsible government which had already been achieved in Canada. He used his

Alfred Waddington was a successful businessman and an early member of the Deluge Engine Company No. 1.   PABC

Left:
These Union Hook and Ladder Company officers, complete with their "leathern" helmets and belts and speaking trumpets posed for a portrait in 1860. They were: (L. to R.:) Edward Ferris, Joseph Wriglesworth, and William Reynolds.

PABC HP12170

The Union Hook and Ladder Company truck in Bastion Square in May 1860. It was steerable from both ends, a useful feature for Victoria's narrow streets.   PABC 7810

A girl of "some six summers" rode the flower bedecked Union Hook and Ladder truck in the 1860 May Day parade. Fire apparatus is still a popular feature of parades today.   PABC HP7816

Right:
Victoria's first fire hall, belonging to the Union Hook and Ladder Co., was a modest affair by today's standards but was touted as magnificent at the time. It was later moved closer to city centre.
VFD

newspaper effectively to rouse, even higher, feelings that already existed within the community.

Many people in Victoria were still unhappy with Douglas' plan for a department, agreeing with De Cosmos that the Hudson's Bay Company was too influential and, in March 1859, there was still talk of forming a properly constituted volunteer department. The editor of the *Colonist* noted that

There has been some talk among businessmen of our town about organizing a fire department. A very commendable project. The idea is, we believe to raise a fund and purchase one of the engines now in possession of the H.B. Co.[9]

There was simply no enthusiasm whatever for the department as organized by Douglas. It was controlled by the *appointed* Police Commissioner, "commanded" by Hudson's Bay employees, and the Company still owned the apparatus. Further proof that the Company connection may have been significant appeared in the *Colonist* a few days later.

Whatever may have been the evils under which this colony has laboured during the proprietorship of the Hudson's Bay Company—now that its claim has lapsed, we should avoid making them perpetual....[10]

While this was a comment on the political situation in Victoria in general, it clearly applied to the formation of the fire department. One feature of American volunteer departments was their independence from established authority, and Douglas' move seemed to be just a continuation of the "old regime." Victoria was suffering from having been a "Company" town from its beginning. However, political consequences aside, it soon became apparent that the existing arrangement simply would not work.

While nothing was really settled regarding the organization of a department, facilities did improve and two cisterns, large underground tanks, were constructed. One was on Store Street, while the other was located on Government Street in the heart of Victoria. The small suction engine could draw water from either of these once they had been filled by the chain gang from the local "gaol." It was fortunate that at least these improvements had been made since the meagre resources of the "fire department" were soon to be tested.

Early in the morning of October 19, 1859, around 4:00 a.m., a major fire broke out and destroyed one of Victoria's largest buildings. It was a frightening experience for all those involved. The *Colonist*, issued later that same morning, carried an account of the fire.

On arriving at the scene of the alarm, the flames were bursting from the east end of the large two storey building on the corner of Government and Johnson streets, owned by Thomas Pattrick and Co. In a short time it was entirely enveloped in fire rendering all efforts to save it from destruction futile—and within an hour it was a smoldering ruin. Mr. Miles who had charge of the establishment and two others, who slept upstairs, were only roused by a sense of suffocation, barely escaping in their night clothes, one party escaping from the window, the other by the stairs, it falling beneath his feet. The Union Hotel...

[9] *Colonist*, 26 March 1859, p. 2.

[10] *Colonist*, 3 June 1859, p. 2.

narrowly escaped entire destruction. At one time the whole side and the lining in the second storey were on fire. The stock and furniture were thrown into the street.

The fire proved to be a frustrating experience for Edward Coker. Those few citizens who did respond to the alarm simply were not willing to obey his orders. Even though he had been appointed a "Chief" of the department by Douglas, the title did not carry with it the necessary, or at least "acceptable," authority. There was nothing personal about it; the problem was that Coker had the misfortune to be the servant of the much disliked Hudson's Bay Company. In any event, despite Coker's best efforts, the attempt to fight the fire was totally chaotic. The press, undoubtedly seizing the opportunity to strike out at the Hudson's Bay Company through Coker, severely criticized what they perceived to be inadequate direction at the fire. They also took the opportunity to cite further pleas for a volunteer department.

Coker, quite justifiably, was upset by the complaints and wrote a letter to the editor of the *Colonist* outlining his grievances. He stated that anyone wishing to assist in fighting a fire would not be prevented from doing so.[11] He was obviously in an impossible position — in charge of a fire department that simply did not exist. Fortunately, he had been able to get marines and sailors from Royal Navy ships at Esquimalt to help out in the absence of any other assistance.

The Pattrick Block fire, apart from all the bad feelings it generated, did have an important result: people were at last upset and worried enough to take significant steps towards creating a fire department, one which would be free of direct Police and Colonial government control. One of those citizens who did respond to the fire alarm wrote to the *Gazette*, and signed himself "Non Sibi Sid Omnibus." The letter appeared in the October 22, 1859, issue of the paper.

I was present at the fire Tuesday morning last, and although I put in some 'big licks' in the way of crying 'fire' until I was hoarse and helped to roll the hose from the reel when we arrived there, having thrown as much mud and whiskey in the fire as anyone in the crowd, and sloshed about in a general way, I was never so dissatisfied with my exertions at a fire before....

Come, gentlemen who are engaged in the collection of subscriptions to start the Victoria Fire Department, let us understand, where we are to stand and how we are to act, but above all don't stand still and let valuable time go by. Get the hooks, ladders, grapnels and axes prepared at once and ready to be used when needed....

As had been the case earlier, it was intended that an American pattern volunteer department would be organized, one in which officers would be elected by the volunteers from among their number. It was a good system and had worked out well in the United States. American inventor and statesman Benjamin Franklin had created the first almost a century earlier in Philadelphia. The great virtue in having the officers elected was that the firefighters had greater confidence in their leaders. Men of ability could rise to the top of the volunteer department and it was in other respects too, well-suited to the times.

At this point, a brief digression is necessary to examine fire-fighting

[11] "Destructive Fire," *Colonist*, 19 October 1859, p. 2.

techniques of the period. These methods were rudimentary and had in fact changed little over the previous century. There had been some improvements in portability and in the quality of parts used in fire engines, but this fact had little influence on fire-fighting techniques. The possibility of putting out a major fire was all but non-existent, and firefighters, like their equivalents even centuries earlier, had to be concerned with preventing the spread of a fire beyond its starting point. This had been the main objective in fighting the Pattrick Block fire where Coker had decided to take what would today be considered both drastic and unacceptable steps. The *Colonist* on the day following the fire reported that

To stop its [the fire's] extension...the house of Mr. I. D. Lowenberg was torn down. Up Johnson Street several small sheds were capsized into the street to prevent its spread in that direction.[12]

It was standard practice in the case of a large blaze to create fire breaks in order to isolate a burning building. The gaps created would, it was hoped, prevent the fire from leaping from one building to the next. This destruction of property was a desperate measure, used only when it was felt that an attempt to put out the fire would fail. In such a circumstance "pull down" hooks and axes were used to bring down a structure if there was time; if not, gunpowder was used to blow it apart, quickly, and thereby create a fire break.

Both these tactics and the technology of fire-fighting required the use of large numbers of men. The operation of manual engines made frequent changes in crews necessary because the men were soon exhausted, and up to 30 men at a time, depending on the type of engine, were needed to man the "brakes" or pump handles, even on a small engine. Pumping crews had to be changed every two or three minutes if an effective stream of water were to be maintained. Often, too, there would be injuries when hands and arms were hit by the rapidly moving handles.

No municipal government could afford to pay the salaries of the large numbers of firefighters needed and even large departments such as those of New York and Chicago were organized as volunteer brigades and took considerable pride in the fact. This being the case, it was inevitable that Victoria as well would create its own department following the pattern established by American volunteer brigades. The first steps were taken with despatch.

"First in order comes the Union... a very swell affair..."
H. E. Levy, Volunteer Fireman

On October 22, 1859, initial steps were taken to organize the first true Victoria volunteer company, the Union Hook and Ladder Co. No. 1. J. J. Southgate and C. W. Wallace were elected by a citizens' committee to solicit funding for a hook and ladder truck and a bell. If someone wanted to join, he would have to support the company financially. This was one of the few requirements but, even so, not everyone was welcome.

The *Colonist*'s colourful editor, Amor De Cosmos, suggested that the committee have at least two French members appointed to it in order to represent that portion of the community.[13] This passed without opposi-

[12] "Fire," *Colonist*, 21 October 1859, p. 2.

[13] "Hook and Ladder Meeting," *Colonist*, 24 October 1859, p. 2.

tion and two individuals were named. But a motion to include "coloureds" on the committee in recognition of their financial support, which had been considerable, was voted down. The Blacks, barred from serving in the fire department, went on to organize one of British Columbia's first military units, the Victoria Pioneer Rifles.

Apart from this one distasteful instance of racial discrimination, it would appear that the fire companies were open to anyone with the means to make a financial contribution. Some members of fire companies were not active participants at all but were really sponsors. Governor Douglas for example, was later made an honorary member of the Deluge Company, contributing his prestige as well as money.

The company rolls for the volunteer fire department show that a broad range of trades and professions were represented: brewers, sailmakers, architects, saddlers, blacksmiths, and barbers to name just a few.[14] The rolls indicate as well that anyone, without regard to his profession or trade, could be elected to officer rank. He was elected by the other firemen and so it was their opinion of him that counted, not his social or financial status.

Hotel keepers seemed to have been well-represented by notable citizens such as Thomas Burnes of Burnes House, and John Keenan, owner of the Fashion Hotel, a popular "watering hole" and dance hall. Keenan particularly was an enthusiastic volunteer fireman having earlier served as one in San Francisco. Some years later, by 1863, he had been elected Chief Engineer of the Victoria department, apparently achieving some renown as the city's "favourite fireman." He was on occasion recognized publicly for his efforts.

In October 1864, a ceremonial speaking trumpet—the ornate versions were used by Chief Engineers everywhere largely as badges of office— was on display at the jewellery store of E. Marks, Yates Street. The trumpet (which is presently in the collection of the B.C. Provincial Museum) had been presented to Keenan by Superintendent Titcomb of San Francisco. Keenan soon after decided to leave Victoria to return to San Francisco and so, according to the *Colonist*

The members of the Victoria Fire Department assembled at the Lyceum Hall for the purpose of presenting a testimonial in the shape of a gold medal to Mr. John C. Keenan, Chief Engineer of the fire department on the occasion of his approaching departure from the colony.

The medal, which is of solid gold, and of excellent workmanship, was manufactured by Mr. E. Watson of Yates Street. It weighs, with the clasp, nearly three ounces and bears on the face of it, the neatly-engraved inscription: Presented to John C. Keenan by the Officers and members of the Victoria Fire Department as a token of respect for his efficient service as chief engineer during the years 1864 and 1865.

On the converse side is a most artistically engraved copy of a chief engineer's hat, surrounded by the words Victoria Fire Department.[15]

It was an emotion-filled evening with Keenan remarking that his memories connected with the department would revive "scenes the most dear on earth." Membership in the department seemed to affect many this way—those fortunate enough to become members that is!

---

[14] Fire Company Rolls, (PABC).

[15] "Presentation," *Colonist*, 14 August 1865, p. 3.

Procedures had been laid down for admitting new members to each company. The *Constitution and Bylaws of the Union Hook and Ladder Co. No. 1* included, as Article 4, the procedure by which candidates were admitted.

Art. 4. There shall be a Standing Committee elected as soon as there are twenty members, and annually thereafter, whose duty it shall be to examine into the qualification and standing of candidates for admission into the Company; and upon their report being favourable, the Company may proceed to an election by ballot, and if such candidate or candidates have THREE negative votes, he or they lose their election.[16]

Earlier, on November 22, 1859, officers were elected by the Union Hook and Ladder Company, and steps had been taken to construct a Hook and Ladder House to accommodate the apparatus which they had ordered from San Francisco. The truck was a first-class type manufactured by Haworth and Ellis of Sacramento. This type of apparatus had been developed in the United States in 1799 to carry the ladders, pulldown hooks, axes and buckets used in fire-fighting. Without a "truck" of this kind, the load would have been almost impossibly cumbersome. Carrying virtually everything required on a single vehicle also meant that tools and other equipment arrived at a fire together, thus dramatically increasing efficiency.

An advertisement requesting tenders to construct the hall for the new company appeared in the *Colonist* under the title "Fire, Fire, Fire." A week before the Hook and Ladder Company had even elected its officers, the *Gazette* reported that plans for the house could be viewed at the office of the architect, John Wright. The structure was to be of two storeys, with a ground area of 20' x 65', and be surmounted by a cupola and bell. In addition to the space needed to store the apparatus, there was to be a meeting room for the company, a feature typical of fire halls elsewhere. Unlike a modern hall, there was no need for "quarters" or living accommodation since the hall on the volunteer system would not be manned on a 24-hour basis. The Hudson's Bay Company agreed to the siting of the House within the compound of the fort for an annual ground rent of one dollar. This was a generous gesture in view of opinions expressed earlier by some residents about the Hudson's Bay Company.

The contract for the construction of the building was awarded to R. Lewis and work proceeded quickly; the foundations had been laid and the walls were going up by the end of December 1859. The April 19, 1860 issue of the *Colonist* announced that the house was being painted and the floor laid and that "the meeting room was to be furnished in a neat and tasty [*sic*] fashion." Manpower was not a problem, with volunteers eager to join the ranks of the independent company coming forward in considerable numbers. In fact, there were enough to form two engine companies just two months later.

The engine companies were formed on essentially the same lines as the Union Hook and Ladder; the first, the Deluge Engine Co. No. 1 on March 5, 1860; and the second, the Tiger Engine Co. No. 2, eighteen days later. Each took over one of the pumpers purchased by the Hudson's Bay Company. They began drills as soon as they had recruited enough

[16] *Constitution and Bylaws of The Union Hook and Ladder Company No. 1*, Victoria, Vancouver Island, 1860, p. 1. (PABC NW 971.83/V 58).

Victoria firefighters used leather New York pattern fire helmets such as this through much of their history. They kept the firefighter safe from falling embers, debris, and water.

1987 JACQUES NOEL JACOBSEN, JR.
COLLECTORS ANTIQUITIES INC.
BY PERMISSION

members to become fully operational, about 65 men each being considered ideal operating strength.[17]

At the outset, financial support for the fire companies was to come from the members themselves or by subscription among the public. Normally, each member contributed $1.00 per month as dues. Honorary members paid $25 each per year, and life members $100 in advance, in order to be able to take part in the company's social activities. Fines were an additional source of revenue and these were charged for non-appearance at a meeting or fire.[18]

There were a number of motives for joining a volunteer fire company, the most obvious being simply a desire to serve the community and not incidentally, to protect one's own property. Also, belonging to the fire department held considerable appeal because of its prominent role within the community. Thomas Deasy, a firefighter from 1869, and by 1889, chief, described how firefighters felt about their role.

Those were great days. There was always energetic rivalry between the two engine companies ... as to which of them should get first water on a fire. The moment the fire bell would ring, we would make a dash for our hall. The first company to arrive received $5 as a prize. But more than the prize, we coveted the honour of being played up in the papers next day.[19]

Uniforms were another inducement to join. Although today firemen still wear uniforms, they are a far cry from the colourful regalia of their predecessors, for each company tried to equal and then outdo the others in splendour. Members of the Union Hook and Ladder, for example, and later other companies, wore attractive uniforms which consisted of red shirts, black trousers, and "leathern" belts which identified them as belonging to a particular company. The shields on their New York pattern helmets also indicated which among its members were officers. Victoria fire companies followed the practice in the United States, choosing inspiring names, distinctive uniforms and insignia which would accentuate the differences between them. There were other, less obvious attractions as well as some that were characteristic of the period.

An important attitude of the Victorian age, and one which was particularly apparent in fire-fighting, has been referred to as the "cult of manliness."[20] The ideal man of the period was expected to be highly masculine, athletic, loyal and brave, and willing to accept discipline without complaint. He was to endure hardship without hesitation and was always ready to demonstrate his physical prowess. It sounds exactly like the qualities a firefighter needed, and represented for many, a major motive for joining a fire company. In fire-fighting for example it was an honour to be placed in the position of greatest danger and this was achieved by being the first to arrive at the engine when an alarm sounded.

With these attitudes, a spirit of competitiveness was inevitable, and in Victoria, this was further increased by Americans in the community joining the Tiger Engine Company No. 2, and the British, becoming members of the Deluge Engine Company No. 1, when they were formed. The competition existing between individuals, and most strikingly, between fire companies, not only proved to be of vital importance in maintaining morale, but it also had a more practical side; it ensured that

[17] It was possible to keep a small manual "engine" working at capacity with 20 men at a time. Having over 60 men available allowed for "shift" changes when fatigue set in.

[18] Hook and Ladder Constitution, p. 2.

[19] "Old Fire Chiefs Recall Vivid Experiences of the Past." *Colonist*, 19 June 1925, p. 21. Mag.

[20] W. L. Morton, "Victorian Canada." in *Shield of Achilles: Aspects of Canada in the Victorian Age.* W. L. Morton, ed. Toronto, McClelland and Stewart, 1968, p. 321.

The Tigers wore "glazed" cloth caps rather than the New York pattern leather helmets sported by their rivals, the Deluge.   PABC HP12168

The Victoria Button pumper was probably identical to this Nanaimo "manual."   BCPM

Amor de Cosmos (Bill Smith) helped establish Victoria's first volunteer fire company—the Union Hook and Ladder.
PABC 2625

Chief Engineer John Keenan had the keys to popularity in early Victoria—he was a capable officer and also owned a saloon.
PABC 3208

"Our Victoria firemen, ever foremost in any public undertaking, have patriotically taken the initiative in preparing to meet His Excellency, Capt. Kennedy, with the honor due his rank." *Colonist*, February 13, 1864.   PABC 7814

Could this photo of a V.F.D. "jumper" have been posed? Some firefighters appear to be pulling hard and others are merely standing, holding on to the wheel.   VFD

the utmost effort was expended in fighting a fire. While this effect was generally to the benefit of the public, things could, and did, go awry on occasion as this incident described by Victoria Chief Joseph Wriglesworth shows.

I remember one night, a bitterly cold one it was, with deep snow on the ground.... there was a big fire on Langley Street in a building owned by Doctor Mathews. The 'Tiger' was the earliest to reach the conflagration and laid hose down the street. A few minutes later, the 'Deluge' arrived and attached the hose to their engine. The men of the 'Tiger' engine, infuriated at such an act, demanded that it should be taken from the Deluge and attached to their engine. The Deluge men refused. Then started such a fight as I've ever seen or participated in. We went at it hammer and tongs, stumbling about in the snow. Nobody thought of the fire. It burned itself out.[21]

By March 21, 1860, Deluge, one of the combatants mentioned above, had recruited 40 men and elected a president, foreman, first assistant foreman, secretary, and treasurer. The term "foreman" was quite appropriate since he was to be in the forefront of the action. The first drill was carried out on the 27th, with the *Colonist* enthusiastically reporting that the Hunneman engine gave "entire satisfaction. The 'old box' worked well and performed some tall squirting."[22]

On May 1, 1860, all three companies took part in the May Day parade led by the band of H.M.S. *Topaz*, a British screw-frigate based at Esquimalt. The Deluge Company, which had decorated its engine with flowers, had the honour of carrying the May Queen, a girl "of some six summers." The Company also carried its own flag before it in the procession. This was a

beautiful satin banner, on the front side of which was inscribed 'Deluge Engine Co. No. 1' with a representation of the Deluge in which appears the 'Ark,' and the last of human race outside of that 'vessel of safety,' clinging to hill tops, rocks, etc., and on the reverse: 'Organized March 5, 1860, We Strive to Save'. There were 59 men headed by three pioneers in blue shirts trimmed with black velvet, black pants, and blue cloth caps. Members of the company itself were dressed in red shirts, with blue badges, black pants and glazed caps.[23]

The Tiger Engine Company No. 2, which unofficially represented the American portion of the community as mentioned, was also present in the parade towing the former San Francisco "Monumental Company" engine, "The Telegraph." The firemen were dressed in their red shirts, leather New York pattern fire helmets, and black pants. Later, on June 23, 1860, the Union Hook and Ladder was presented with a blue and white flag made by the ladies of Victoria, the device on the banner being, appropriately, a crossed hook and ladder.

Impressed by the colourful Deluge and Union banners, and not about to be outdone, the Tigers, shortly before the next year's May Day parade, took possession of a flag bearing the likeness of a Bengal Tiger. They proudly accepted the gift from the hand of the Governor's daughter, Agnes Douglas. The Company's motto "Our Aim, the Public Good" was also prominently displayed on the flag. That year all three companies were inspected by the Governor in the afternoon following the parade. Slowly, progress was being made towards providing the organization,

[21] "Old Fire Chiefs...", *Colonist*, 19 June 1925, p. 21.

[22] *Colonist*, 24 March 1860, p. 2.

[23] *Colonist*, 28 April 1860, p. 2.

equipment and personnel for effective fire-fighting in Victoria.

While the means of raising an alarm was primitive in a small town like Victoria, it worked well. Simply shouting or running to the nearest fire hall and ringing its bell was enough to bring the firemen on the run. Members of the department would drop what they were doing and dash to their engines. On occasion this could be disturbing to those not familiar with volunteer departments as this account appearing in the *Colonist* indicates:

In the '70s, a noted lecturer spoke in the Theatre Royal. The fire bells rang, and in five minutes, there were not twenty-five left in the audience. The speaker stopped and indignantly said he had never been so slighted. One of the audience rose and appealed to the lecturer. 'Do you know, Sir, that many of those who left are firemen, and their house may have been the one on fire? Do you know that each was liable to be fined for non-attendance at a fire.' The lecturer, on this apologized and proceeded with the lecture.[24]

Now that the fire companies were in operation, the time had come to "fine tune" things for the sake of efficiency. The elected foremen of the three companies were requested to attend a meeting called by the president of the Legislative Council for noon on July 12, 1860. Over the course of the meeting, the representatives were questioned at considerable length on matters relating to fire protection. The legislators, in contrast to their earlier lethargy, moved quickly. The result was the third reading and passing into law of the Fireman's Protection Act, 1860, which was enacted on the 20th of that month.[25]

This act, the first law dealing with fire protection in British Columbia, was an important and basic step because it provided necessary legal protection against charges of wilful damage to private property by firemen in the course of their duty. As seen in the case of the Pattrick Block fire, even property not already on fire could be destroyed in order to prevent the blaze from spreading. If hard feelings had existed previously between the property owner and the fireman, the latter could well have found himself facing charges without this legislation no matter how legitimate his actions. Taking this sort of precaution was already a feature of fire protection elsewhere. Being now well-established, the firefighters were soon to find themselves part of a more regulated, co-ordinated department.

Co-ordination of fire-fighting effort was still a problem that had to be addressed. What existed at this time—the three independent companies —could not properly be termed a fire department because their activities lacked co-ordination above the company level. Companies could find themselves competing to the detriment of the task at hand. Chaos could and did, on occasion, result at a fire. A chief engineer (once again the American terminology was used) was needed to be in charge of the department and of fighting fires. He was to be the equivalent of the modern fire chief and so all companies were to come under his command in action.

An amended version of the Act was approved on September 11, 1861, which provided for the creation of a Board of Delegates to serve as the governing body of the Victoria Fire Department. Both the delegates and officers sitting on this board were elected by the companies from among

[24] "Victoria's Firemen Fifty Years Ago." *Colonist*, 7 February 1923, p. 3.

[25] *Minutes of the Council of Vancouver Island, Commencing August 30th, 1851, and Terminating with the Prorogation of the House of Assembly, February 6th 1861.* Victoria, King's Printer, 1918., p. 65. (Archives of British Columbia Memoire No. 11).

their own members. In this way, the department retained its democratic form.

In keeping with this, the chief engineer who was at first elected by the delegates and, by 1886, by the ratepayers, was responsible to the Governor. He was required to submit an annual report describing the activities of the department. This report included an inventory of apparatus and equipment, a roster of members, a list of fires attended recording the loss involved in each as well as the cause where known. Of great importance, he included as well recommendations to improve the department. James McRae was elected as Victoria's first chief engineer. The Act also made official the department's control of its internal affairs, subject to approval by the governor.

From that point on, the Hudson's Bay Company had nothing to do with the operation of the department, and by 1865, the two engines purchased by them earlier became the property of the Tiger and Deluge companies. In 1872, when costs had escalated to a point where they were too high for the individual companies to cope with alone, all three companies turned their property over to the department. It, in turn, was to seek funding either from the public, the insurance companies by taxation, the Colonial government then later, the provincial government, or the city, which had been incorporated in 1862. Financial problems continued to plague the department throughout the volunteer era.

By 1863, the burden of paying dues and fines, supplying uniforms and otherwise supporting the companies, became too heavy for many individual volunteer firefighters, and the department began to lose members. What could be done to reverse the trend? The answer was not long in coming. Jury duty, in the 1860s as now, was usually viewed with something less than enthusiasm, and so it was proposed by the firefighters, in view of the valuable public service performed by them without compensation, that they should be exempted to some degree from sitting on juries. In the opinion of many, the exemption from jury duty would compensate for the expense of belonging to the department.

This proposal was acceptable with one omission, that there was to be no exemption from Coroner's juries, and it was enacted as an amendment to the Fireman's Protection Act, 1864, to which assent was given on July 7.[26] But there was one potential problem that could result: too many firemen, and too few available jurors! Jury duty was frequent in a small town like Victoria; there were simply too few people qualified to sit. Steps had to be taken to ensure that the size of the fire companies was limited and the supply of jurors adequate. While the manpower problems were being solved, thereby gaining some relief from financial problems, new equipment had to be purchased and this involved special efforts to raise money.

Major expenses, such as buying apparatus and equipment were usually met by subscription from the community at large, and the insurance companies. Both obviously stood to benefit from improved fire protection. Donations were seldom adequate to the task, however, and the Board of Delegates were forced to approach Governor Douglas in May 1862. The old Rodgers engine, the "Telegraph," which was purchased used, was by this time all but totally worn out. The department pressed its

26 James E. Hendrickson, ed. *Journals of the Colonial Legislatures of Vancouver Island and British Columbia.* Victoria, Provincial Archives of British Columbia, 1980. (Volume III, *Journals of the House of Assembly, Vancouver Island, 1863-1866,* p. 159.

case strongly: the Chief Engineer, J. A. McCrae, in correspondence with Douglas on May 20, 1862, noted

... the necessity of immediate action in this matter, as our town is fast filling up with wooden buildings, and we are liable at any moment to a conflagration, that would be beyond the power of the department to subdue.[27]

The House of Assembly appropriated funds for a new Button and Blake manual engine which was ordered from A. H. Titcomb of San Francisco. This was the second appropriation for the department in 1862; the first was to cover general expenses and hose. The engine proved to be an instant success when it arrived in September, but the same cannot be said for the financial arrangements and the Tigers had to approach the government once again to make up the shortfall. Other means had to be devised.

Social events such as balls, while very pleasant, and in any case part of the department's social life, acquired a more important function: they became a popular and reasonably effective means of raising money. A fireman's diary relates that on

December 31st, 1872. Fireman's Ball took place in the Alhambra Hall and was a perfect success. Total receipts $266.00, expenses $200.84½ leaving a balance of $65.12½ which was divided among the three companies.[28]

Picnics were another means of raising funds, and were attended enthusiastically by the public. A lengthy description of the event would usually appear in the newspaper the following day. This account appeared in the *Colonist* on July 27, 1868:

The pic-nic given at Cadboro Bay yesterday under the auspices of the Tiger Engine Company, was the pic-nic *par excellence* of the season. At half-past ten o'clock the company paraded at their engine house, and preceded by the band of the Rifle Corps, in firemens' uniform, marched with their apparatus through the city. On the hose cart stood a real genuine tiger, with glaring eye balls, though a nearer approach revealed the reassuring fact that the animal was stuffed with straw. At about eleven o'clock the pleasure seekers commenced leaving town in every description of vehicle capable of running on four wheels or two for the scene of attraction. Williams' mammoth buss [*sic*] "Young America" was of course at a premium, and with other coaches was kept travelling to and fro ... at one o'clock the majority of pic-nicers were on the ground and a beautiful sight it was to witness the gaily dressed groups interspersed with the scarlet shirts of the firemen congregated on the grassy slopes of that most romantic and picturesque spot.... Not far distant stood a handsomely ornamented refreshment bar presided over by mine host of the "Crooked Billet", where iced beverages, "lager", and other enticing liquids were dispensed, and secretary Holden had charge of the tables containing the equally necessary appendages to rustic enjoyment—the eatables.

While these affairs were obviously enjoyed and undoubtedly did help the "Exchequer" of the companies, more formalized and legally enforceable means of raising money for capital expenses were devised. Laws which required the insurance companies operating in Victoria to support the fire companies were enacted. An "ordinance to enable the Municipal Council of the City of Victoria to establish a permanent fund for the support of the fire establishments..." was signed by Governor Frederick Seymour on March 11, 1868.

[27] Petition to Governor Douglas, 20 May 1862, (PABC/C.O./F494-3).

[28] *Fireman's Diary*, (PABC 81-94), unpaged.

This law, known as the *Fire Companies Aid Act*, signified for the first time the attempt by the city to ensure that fire protection was, at least in part, supported financially.[29] It did not, however, indicate that the city itself was assuming responsibility for financing the department — that would not happen until 1886. The members of the department were still primarily responsible for its survival. Apparatus and equipment purchases were frequent.

In September 1863, two locally-built hose carts were purchased at a cost of $250 each.[30] Manufactured by Bunting and Dodds of Yates Street, one went to the Tigers and the other to the Deluge. Leather fire buckets, useful where there was not enough water available to supply a pumper, were also being produced in Victoria at this time. Fire hose in use in the 1860s and later was cumbersome and chief engineers, because they had to use it, were very particular as to which type was purchased. Chief Engineer John Keenan, for example, was very specific as to which materials he would not tolerate: "Gutta Percha, Web (wrapped in twine) Hemp, Canvass, California Hose, and a variety of single rivetted hose."[31] Significantly, good quality hose, able to withstand higher pressures, would be even more necessary in the near future as new apparatus, the first of its type west of Toronto, would soon become part of the Victoria Fire Department's roster.

THE STANDARD TRADE MARK.

OAK LEATHER HOSE.

[29] Hendrickson, *op. cit*, volume V, p. 261.

[30] "Hose Carts," *Colonist*, 8 September 1863, p. 3.

[31] John Keenan, *Annual Report of the Fire Department ending June 30th 1865*, p. 10. (PABC G/V66/V66x).

Chapter 2

STEAM SQUIRTS: VICTORIA BUYS THE BEST

The world's first steam fire engine, a very rudimentary affair, was produced in England by Braithwaite and Ericsson in 1829-30. While this machine did work, it took several years—decades really—before steam pumpers could prove themselves both sufficiently advantageous, and reliable, to win acceptance. The development of steam fire apparatus lagged behind that of ships' engines, railway locomotives, and stationary plants. The problem was in making heavy, cumbersome steam-powered pumps portable. By the early 1860s, steam-powered fire apparatus was becoming increasingly efficient, more readily available and, as a consequence, more desirable.

During this period of transition from hand to mechanical pumpers, steam and manual engines both inevitably had their advocates. Those supporting the hand-powered pumpers claimed that they were superior because they could be brought into action faster. This was true since there was no need to wait until steam pressure reached an operating level. These enthusiasts, and there were many, also felt that it was somehow an affront to their manhood to use steam power. This attitude is hardly surprising in view of the heroic attitudes of the period. However, a Victoria steam enthusiast writing in the *Colonist* on December 14, 1867, pointed out the arguments held by other enthuiasts elsewhere, when he noted that:

... a steam engine, well fed with fuel and water never stops work from fatigue—a man does, when overworked, be he ever so well fed. A steam fire engine, costing $3,000 laid down here, would probably perform more service than six of the best hand engines ever made, manned by 300 men, and by pouring two or more steady streams upon a burning building would drown out any fire of reasonable size that is likely to break out here for a number of years.[1]

One effect the introduction of steam pumpers had in larger centres such as New York and Chicago, was to dramatically reduce manpower requirements. The steamers had a far greater capacity than their manual equivalents with one or two men and a steamer replacing 50 or 60 men with a manual engine. In much larger cities than Victoria the introduction of steam pumpers led directly to professional, paid departments. Even with the higher initial cost of the apparatus, it was a reasonable proposition to pay firefighters given the lower manpower requirements and the greater skills needed to operate the steam apparatus.

Though there was at this time no possibility of a professional department in Victoria, steam fire-fighting captured the imagination of the

[1] "Wanted—A Steam Pumper," *Colonist*, 14 December 1867, p. 1.

volunteer firefighters. The Tigers ordered a steam pumper from Button
and Blake of Waterford, New York, the same company that had manufactured the Tigers' manual engine in 1862. By coincidence, Button began
manufacturing steamers in the same year the Victoria hand engine was
delivered. Their first steamer, which proved very successful, was sold to
Battle Creek, Michigan. Lysander Button himself took considerable
pride in the state-of-the-art pumper delivered to Victoria, referring to it in
a letter to Frank Sylvester, Secretary of the Tigers, as "as good a steamer
as ever was built." The engine was shipped from New York in October
and it arrived in December 1868. The costs were substantial for the time.

Cost:	$3,900.00
Freight: N.Y.-San Francisco	642.55
San Francisco-Victoria	121.20
Collections Charges:	24.40
Fitting up:	60.00
Contingent Expenses:	310.25
Total	$5,042.25[2]

The Tiger Company celebrated the arrival of their new engine in
December 1868 with a party, the cost of which was cited as being $147.75
for alcoholic refreshment and $150.00 for dinner. Fortunately, no fires
seem to have occurred while the party was underway. The steamer itself
performed magnificently when tested, proving capable of throwing two
streams of water around 140 feet at 120 lb. pressure, and at 80 lb. pressure,
it could throw a single stream 200 feet. From a cold start, the engine could
be ready for action in about eight minutes.[3]

The Tigers themselves contributed $1,000, and public subscriptions
evidently raised $1,471.50, with insurance companies being major con-
tributors.[4] There was still a shortfall, and at the request of the Tigers, the
government contributed $750, while Governor Kennedy, who had suc-
ceeded Douglas in 1864, allowed the engine to enter the colony duty free,
a gesture which amounted to a major contribution.

The Deluge, very impressed with the performance of the Tigers' engine
and, once again not to be outdone by its rivals, was also actively
considering the purchase of a steamer. The *Colonist* of February 16, 1869,
reported that

the Deluge Fire Engine Company of this city, we understand, contemplate
procuring a steam fire engine from London if sufficient encouragement be
extended them by the Government, the insurance agents and property holders.
The result of recent successful trials of the Tiger Steam Engine so completely
outdid all that was ever effected by hand engines as to literally leave no
comparison between the two classes: and we are not surprised that our citizens
have commenced to contemplate with a feeling of insecurity and alarm, the
possibility of a conflagration occurring—and a calamity of the kind might occur
at any moment—and finding them dependent upon but two engines, one of them
worked by hand. The English steamers took the prize at a trial in London with
two American steamers, and the cost (Mr. Waddington has written out) is one
third less than those furnished by any other country.

The Deluge went ahead with their plans, acquiring an English Merryweather steamer in April 1870. They successfully tapped the same sources

[2] (PABC G/V66/V66a) The price of $3900.00
was in "Greenbacks," then worth $0.73
Canadian—for once, things worked out in
our favour!

[3] *Colonist*, 21 December 1868, p. 2.

[4] *Colonist*, 20 December 1867, p. 1. "The
Insurance Companies have already indicated
their intention to 'act most liberally,' Mr.
Wigham of the Royal giving $300.00 and
Mr. R. J. Stewart for the companies of
which he was an agent, $200."

for funding as the Tigers, raising the $2,658.26 required.[5] This price, paid to Sproat and Company as agents, included the usual freight, fitting up and test charges. With the Deluge buying an English engine, and the Tigers, an American, it would seem that the national rivalries were still present if less obvious. In any case, the test of the new Deluge engine proved it to be an excellent machine as the *Colonist* reported on April 26, 1870:

The whistle was blown at three minutes 1 second, 20 lbs. of steam were raised in 9½ minutes and water thrown. In 13 minutes 30 seconds there were 60 lbs. of steam, and with 100 lbs. of steam, two powerful streams of water were thrown through inch nozzles many feet—some estimate 40—above the St. Nicholas Hotel staff.

Six of the younger members of each engine company were soon trained to act as engineers for the steam engines. Among this fortunate group was H. E. Levy, a prominent Victoria restauranteur and enthusiastic volunteer firefighter.

The insurance companies, though asked to contribute with some frequency to drives to purchase new apparatus, were well aware of the valuable service performed by the fire companies, and on occasion demonstrated their gratitude and encouragement with donations in addition to those required by law. The same diary cited earlier regarding the firemen's ball also recorded that

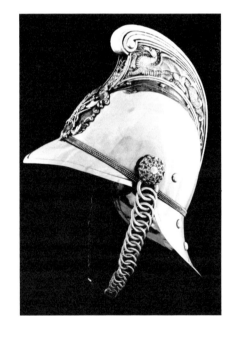

Mr. T. C. Nuttall, agent for the Phoenix Insurance Company presented the department with $50.00 for their services and efficiency at the above fire (22 January 1873) at the Mountain Saloon; Total loss $1000. (Tigers—first water)[6]

Even though required by law to support the department, the insurance companies were astute enough to realize that rewards such as this might well inspire greater efforts by the firefighters. There were to be additional inducements provided as well, such as the presentation of an ornate London Fire Brigade style helmet to Chief C. J. Phillips in 1885 by the Guardian Fire Insurance Company of London. It was appropriately inscribed, complimenting him for his outstanding service in providing fire protection. Tokens such as this were important in terms of inspiring greater effort, and from the early 1860s, that effort had been necessary. Now a new threat emerged.

"Incendiaries": Villains are on the loose!

As Victoria's population increased as a result of the Fraser and Cariboo gold rushes of the late 1850s and early 1860s, incidents of arson also increased in number. Apparently an unknown "villain" made an attempt on the outhouse attached to the home of a Mr. Davis in November 1858 — one can hope that the gentleman concerned was not using it at the time. In this incident, as in so many cases of arson during this period, the sole object of the incendiary appeared to the citizens to be the destruction of the town. Since this was the generally accepted result of any fire, only someone bent on the town's destruction could deliberately set a blaze. There is a plea in the same newspaper article reporting the incident that

[5] "An English Steam Fire Engine." *Colonist*, 16 February 1869, p. 3.

[6] Fireman's Diary, (PABC 81-94).

citizens be on the alert against "suspicious" characters. This was apparently the second incident of arson reported to the paper.

The increasing expense entailed in paying claims for fires, some of which were undoubtedly of incendiary origin, provoked the insurance companies to seek some means of dealing with "incendiarism" — the term "arson" appears not to have been in use at that time. The *Journal of the Legislative Council of British Columbia* contains a reference to a petition from "sundry insurance agents and merchants in Victoria" submitted to the council on April 16, 1868.[7]

Twelve days later, the petition was presented to the Governor and passed as the *Fire Enquiry Ordinance 1868*, which "clothed" magistrates throughout the colony with powers to hold inquests upon fires. Fire investigation was in its infancy and it would undoubtedly have been difficult to prove criminal intent in at least the majority of cases. It was, and in fact still is, difficult to prove someone guilty of arson. Nevertheless, this legislation may have deterred some would-be arsonists.

The object of arsonists would in any case be more difficult to accomplish with the fire department organized, but another, and equally fundamental inadequacy — the water supply — had to be rectified before fire protection could be considered satisfactory. Little had been accomplished in this regard since Douglas' earlier and largely unsuccessful attempts.

In previous years, cisterns, or underground storage reservoirs, which could hold sizeable quantities of fresh water until needed, appeared to be the best solution for at least the fire-fighting supply. But whose responsibility was it to pay for such necessary projects? The means of collecting revenue was not fully developed. The Corporation of Victoria, the municipal government, would not come into being until 1862. One citizen, possibly a member of one of the original fire companies of 1858, wrote to the *Gazette* that

... after the noble and generous action taken by a few old residents of Victoria, after the Liberal and intelligent support of our Governor in carrying through the urgent measure for prevention and extinguishment of fires, it is to [be] regretted that subsequent steps should be so dilatory in the matter of constructing cisterns. It is mortifying to think that we have sent a petition to the Governor, which was immediately acceeded [*sic*] to, and that after obtaining the desired permission to go on with the work, we should in effect abandon the most important portion of the project — the construction of the cisterns....[8]

Alfred Waddington, a Victoria merchant and later, a member of the Deluge, had himself paid for the construction of the first cistern near his business at Waddington Alley and Store Street, thereby guaranteeing that he at least would be certain of water in the event of fire. Some years later, in a *Colonist* interview, Joseph Wriglesworth recalled an incident surrounding the construction of the second cistern.

There was another cistern built a little later, and the contract for excavating was let to a Negro by the name of William Bond, who had been a slave at one time. Some practical joker wanted to have some fun at Bond's expense, and went up to the excavation one night and put a lot of brass filings in the earth.

In the morning when the negro arrived on the scene and saw the glint of metal he believed that he had struck a gold mine. It was in the days of gold excitement. He

[7] Hendrickson, *Journals of the Executive Council of the Colony of Vancouver Island*, Volume IV, p. 162.

[8] "The Cisterns and the Fire Companies." *Weekly Gazette*, 14 August 1858, p. 4.

made his two workers swear to absolute secrecy, and between the three of them they carted every bit of earth out of the hole to Bond's yard some blocks away, to be washed for precious metals.[9]

A subscription had been taken up among members of the business community to pay for the construction of the second cistern. While today little is known of these tanks at least in terms of their structure, it is safe to assume that they were essentially underground tanks with brick or wood walls and bottoms, and wooden lids, part of which could be lifted for filling or for use by the fire department. On at least one occasion it is recorded that following a fire, a visitor to the town who had the temerity to criticize the department, was soon forced by the irate firefighters to inspect one at claustrophobically close quarters. Initially, the tanks were filled by the chain gang. The two tanks, while of some use, were far from what was needed and it was still uncertain how the others would be paid for and arrangements made for construction.

Lack of immediate action by the Colonial Assembly had resulted in private initiative filling the void and building the first two cisterns. No further construction had taken place by November 1860 when "A Citizen" wrote an outraged letter to the editor of the *Colonist*. He was upset by the fact that a third cistern, the funds for which had been voted by the Legislature in January 1859, still had not been constructed.

When your correspondent pays the taxes which the house voted so readily, without even waiting to obtain the equivalents of self-government and representation, he will find that, on that score at least they have been less lazy than he thought . . .[10]

The writer went on to criticize the citizens of Victoria for their apparent apathy and suggested that it would be very easy for a number of them to get together and construct the necessary cisterns themselves. However, in his view, the example of laziness set by the government was undoubtedly too pervasive to expect this to happen in spite of the earlier efforts. The letter indicates a growing feeling among some citizens that the government was delinquent in a role it should have been fulfilling.

While raising funds by subscription for public works succeeded on a small scale in this instance because there was really no alternative, it is clear that any attempt to do so for larger projects would result in failure. Some other means of raising revenue for public projects had to be devised. The solution to the problem was taxation. The first instance of its being used appears to have been to pay for much-needed road improvements rather than the equally necessary cisterns. An Act of August 28, 1860, levied a tax of five eighths per cent on all real estate to pay for road work. Taxation was initially not a popular means of raising funds, even with the government, partly because of the difficulties inherent in administering it.

Four years later, road work was still being supported by indirect taxation such as through customs duties which were levied on all imports, a method suggested by the British government. The Colonial Office, the government body responsible, was loath to appropriate the $10,000 requested by Victoria for "public works," feeling that it should be raised locally.[11] Obviously, as the size of the community grew, so too did the

[9] "Old Fire Chiefs...", *Colonist*, 19 June 1925, p. 21.

[10] "About Cisterns and Other Things," *Colonist*, 1 November 1860, p. 3.

[11] F. E. Walden, *The Social History of Victoria, B.C.: 1858-1871* (unpublished B.A. Essay. University of British Columbia, 16 April 1951), p. 66.

Left:
The Tigers' Button and Blake steamer
had a "squirrel tail" hard suction hose.
PABC 12911

Below:
This early 1880s view from the Songhees
reserve shows a growing city. Hudson's
Bay Company ships are tied up at the
Enterprise Wharf on the right.
PABC 68483

The Deluge Co. members showed obvious pride in their new Merryweather pumper. Smaller than the Tiger engine, the Deluge had an elegant wood lagged boiler.   VFD

The Deluge opened their last hall with considerable fanfare with the other fire companies joining in. This photo was taken from a nearby bakery roof.

PABC 12165

Joseph Wriglesworth, shown here surrounded by the tools of the trade, was Victoria's first true fire chief. He was in charge of all three companies—The Tigers, The Deluge, and The Union Hook and Ladder.   PABC 7823

need for more and larger publicly-funded projects. This situation led to the successful agitation for a second level of government — the municipal corporation — which was finally established in 1862.

The problem of providing water for fire-fighting was, as noted, tied to the need for an adequate supply for all uses, and could be the cause of controversy. In one instance, for example, an attempt was apparently made to monopolize the fresh water supply in Victoria. The *Colonist* of April 29, 1861, protested that

> Attorney-General Cary, we learn from good authority, is the party who purchased the property from the Hudson's Bay Company.... The friends of would be water monopolists assert that a company will be formed, pipes laid, and that element brought into our houses. This sounds very well. We are thinking however, that monopolists have been pipe laying for so long that their stock will be exhausted before they even obtain possession of the property.

Colonist editor Amor De Cosmos, a self-proclaimed guardian of the public, took the government to task. Meanwhile others, not connected to the government were busy.

In April 1863, a Bill placed before the Legislature by two Victoria entrepreneurs Messrs. Martin and Coe, to supply water to Victoria from artesian wells at Spring Ridge, was unsuccessful. This company had failed in its attempt to convince a committee of the legislature that enough water was available from the source to make their scheme practical. The company had, however, established the rudiments of the facilities and run a line into the centre of the town by March 1864 despite the lack of legislative authority.

The Spring Ridge Water Works Co. Ltd. bought out Martin and Coe in September 1864, and subsequently went to considerable effort to explain that the service had been less than adequate because of a water shortage brought about by extreme drought. Wells in the city had gone dry and consequently increased the burden on their facilities. Because Martin and Coe had been refused a charter, necessary works to correct the problem had not been completed.

This situation, the absence of operating and effective water works, directly affected the ability of the fire department to fight fires. The cisterns, which the water company had agreed to keep filled via underground mains, went dry. At this time twelve-foot-long hollowed logs, reinforced by wire, carried the water. In November 1864, after a major fire, Chief Engineer John Keenan, severely criticized the water company, reminding the citizens of Victoria that because a cistern had been allowed to run dry, they had nearly lost the Victoria theatre a month earlier.[12] Fortunately, the fire was extinguished.

This fire, which had been caused by the upset of a camphene lantern, could very well have destroyed the theatre. Even before this incident, Keenan had somewhat prophetically taken the water company to task in a letter to A. E. Kennedy, the Colonial Secretary, outlining his complaints in some detail.[13] This apparently had little effect because the service was still inadequate four years later. An editorial appearing in December 1868 pointed out that water could easily be piped from a lake, only six miles from the city. In the words of the editor, "It is a duty

Iron water mains were a great improvement over the hollowed logs first used to carry water.

[12] "A Card to the Public," *Colonist*, 10 September 1864, p. 2.

[13] J. C. Keenan to A. E. Kennedy. 29 October 1864 (PABC/C.O./F860-4).

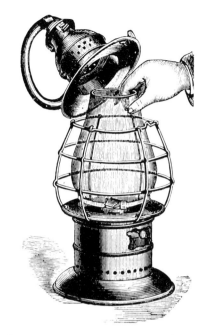

Lanterns were very necessary in fire-fighting.

incumbent on the Government" to provide the city with proper water. Nothing was done, and four years later, in 1872, the government's chief engineer, Thomas Bulkley, reported that it would be easy to establish a water system capable of supplying a town of 90,000 inhabitants from underground mains. The necessary funds were raised by means of the sale of municipal debentures, and the Victoria Water Works began operation in August 1875.[14]

It was fortunate that the new water works were by this time operational, because a fire occurred at the Spring Ridge water works just before noon on August 5, 1875 which totally destroyed the plant. It was a bad day for the fire department as well: the Deluge hand engine rolled over on Pandora Avenue at Blanshard near the Synagogue while on the way to the fire, and the Union Hook and Ladder truck was involved in a collision on Yates while en route to the same fire.

With the new water works, the city had a reliable, potentially plentiful supply of water. The first hydrants for fire department use were in service by 1877 and their number was increased throughout the years as the mains spread out to include new areas of the city. However, even with mains and hydrants, the cisterns still proved useful on occasion. The *Colonist* reported on December 4, 1880 that a cistern was pressed into service when smoke was spotted issuing from the upper storey of the new post office building.

Difficulty was experienced for some time in obtaining water from private pipes as most of the taps had been frozen by the severity of Thursday night. An alarm was consequently sounded and the engines of the department being quickly on the spot, water was obtained from the tank at the intersection of Government and Yates Streets.

To ensure that the lids on the tanks would not freeze shut in the winter, Chief Phillips had wisely taken the precaution of salting the joints. The system of employing cisterns for fire department use was perpetuated and extended until 1908, when a high-pressure salt water system was introduced in the central business district. Before that time, the water pressure was not sufficient in the mains to keep hydrants operational and tanks from which the engines would pump water had to be kept filled for emergency use. There were 13 tanks in use in the city when the use of cisterns was finally discontinued. The salt water system had a limitless supply—the harbour.

Taking Care: A Legal Necessity

With the creation of an effective fire department and the assurance that adequate water would be available, it was reasonably certain that fires could now be suppressed. The department did not in 1860 have the authority to require that precautions be taken against fire. The *Colonist* was well aware of the problem and once again complained in print in June 1861.

If there exists no precise statute to authorize it [the enactment and means to enforce fire codes] it should be done by the Government under the statute of common consent, for the common protection of everybody's property.

[14] Thomas Bulkley, *The Victoria Water Supply: Report to the Commissioner of Lands and Works, Victoria, British Columbia Dated 28 October 1872.* Victoria, *Daily Standard,* 1872, P. 18.

The first attempt to restrict unsafe practices and provide the means to enforce precautions had, as mentioned, appeared in the Grand Jury Report of January 1859. New fire limits legislation—what we would today refer to as fire codes—represented what was for the time a thorough approach to fire precaution.

Once enacted, it was hoped, such considerations as the mounting of stovepipes, the size and disposition of wooden buildings and the separation of hazardous trades or businesses from each other and residences would all be regulated. Increased pressure was brought to bear by the public to have the Colonial government take action. For some time, it was uncertain which level of government—colonial or municipal—should be responsible for setting and expanding fire limits, those areas in which fire protection would be provided and laws enforced, within the city.

The *Colonist* correctly stated that a municipal ordinance would be the most efficient solution, since an act of the Legislature would require the approval of the Colonial Office in London, a cumbersome and time-consuming arrangement. Common sense prevailed and with the creation of the municipal corporation, legislation governing fire limits became the city's responsibility. The first Fire Limits Bill passed City Council and became law on July 12, 1862, establishing standards to be enforced within specified geographical limits and providing as well the means for inspection and enforcement. The act stated that

Thenceforth no person will be permitted to erect any wooden building more than eighteen feet high, and not more than one storey, within the limits bounded by Johnson St. on the north, the west side of Broad St, on the east, and the north side of the harbor on the west.[15]

Exactly seventeen months later, the city was divided into wards for administrative purposes. Each was assigned a number, and by means of the tower bell striking an appropriate number of times, the location of the fire could be quickly identified by the volunteers. Later, from the late 1870s, the system was continued using the city hall bell in the same manner with the phone company activating the signal. The legal or legislative basis upon which fire protection could be provided had been established, but there were still improvements of an equally important nature that had to be introduced. Hints of what was coming—horse drawn apparatus—appeared in the press in the early 1870s.

The growth of Victoria also meant that a larger area had to be protected, and this situation created a significant problem for the firefighters. Like their equivalents in larger cities, they had to cope with ever-increasing distances to travel. Fire apparatus at this time was towed by firefighters themselves with the inevitable result that crews arrived at a fire already exhausted. The steam pumpers were designed to be hand-towed, a tough job, particularly if road surfaces were anything less than ideal. The fact that this was an increasingly serious problem is indicated by this letter published in the *Colonist* on August 9, 1873, describing a serious fire on the outskirts of the town.

The extended city limits revive the question of how the department can be supplied with locomotive power for their engines. It is rather too much to expect

[15] "Fire Limits Bill a Law," *Colonist*, 12 July 1862, p. 3.

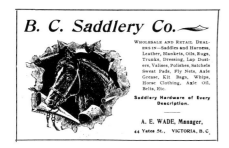

the firemen to do their work efficiently at a fire when they have been used up as beasts of burden dragging their engines along newly gravelled or sandy roads long distances. The fire yesterday was an illustration of what we advance. When orders were given to unlimber, some of the men dropped on the ground completely exhausted with the running and hauling—the remainder being anything but up to their work. That this is an unsatisfactory state of affairs is only too self-evident—painfully so to the firemen themselves. It were time that this department made some arrangement with the livery stable keepers to have a horse handy—harnessed every night for the service respectively of each company.

As if to make the point, there was a second fire that same day, occurring at 2:00 a.m. That same issue of the *Colonist* reported that

About 2 o'clock yesterday morning a fire broke out in a frame building used as a tannery by Mr. W. G. Norris and situated on Dallas Street. The building, which contained a considerable quantity of goods, was entirely consumed 'ere the fire companies arrived with their engines. The Hook and Ladder Company took up the planking of the sidewalks nearby and beat out the fire which was spreading through the bush. The Deluge got their hose to a neighboring well and threw some water, but not in time to do any good. The insurance with the "Phoenix" was for $800, far short of the value of the property destroyed.

A bucket company had been formed three years earlier in December 1870, and had been attached to the Union Hook and Ladder. It was undoubtedly these people who had helped prevent the spread of the tannery fire. A number of fires occurring in a short interval created serious problems for the firefighters. Had horses been available to tow the apparatus, fatigue resulting from having to fight two fires would have been less of a problem for the firefighters. Though the value of horses was recognized, their use in Victoria at least was not introduced until 1880, largely because of the expense involved in providing the animals with 24-hour care and food. Attempts to provide horses on an as-required basis from local livery stables simply did not work out, this arrangement proving to be both too cumbersome and expensive. When the decision was made to have horses on strength to haul at least the heavy steam pumpers, paid stewards had to be introduced to ensure that both the animals and fire halls were well-cared for. There had in fact been considerable changes in the accommodation provided for the apparatus over the years.

Fire Halls

As noted, all fire apparatus was initially stored in the Fort, but once the fire companies were organized as volunteers, it was removed to quarters used by the respective companies. This was significant, in that some degree of independence could be achieved from the Hudson's Bay Company. In April 1860, the Deluge engine was temporarily removed from the house near the fort "to the room lately occupied by E. Mallandine's School, on Broad Street. Members of the Company will take notice, and remember to find their machine in case of alarm until after the [May Day] parade."[16] Deluge then moved into a building on Government Street between Yates and Johnson, and the Tigers established their headquarters around the corner on the same block between Government and Broad streets.

[16] "Removal of the Deluge Engine," *Colonist*, 26 April 1860, p. 2.

The President of the Tigers, T. H. McCann, made their move into quarters "official" by purchasing a large flagpole formerly situated in front of the American Hotel. Steamboat captain Alexander Murray donated a large flag, undoubtedly a Union Jack of the prodigous dimensions common in the nineteenth century. For a time, Deluge lost its quarters and was forced to store its apparatus, first in its rivals', the Tigers, and then in the Union Hook and Ladder house. By late April 1863, however, the company was able to lease property on Yates Street and build a hall which was to serve it for 14 years. The *Colonist* of April 23, 1863, carried an excellent description of the opening festivities.

The capacious Engine Room was elegantly fitted up for the occasion. At the lower end of the room the various banners of the company were tastefully displayed with wreaths of flowers and supported by the material flags of Great Britain and the United States while on the walls around hung pictures illustrative of the life of a fireman, and miniature 'Jacks' and 'Stars and Stripes'. At 8 o'clock the company alarm bell began to ring vigorously, announcing the approach of the firemen with the company's engine. On reaching the building the engine was pulled up to the door and the firemen and their friends proceeded to regale themselves on the excellent refreshments set before them. 'Success to the Deluge Co. No. 1' was drunk in a bumper with three times three, followed by the health of Chief Engineer, Mr. John Dickson, the Foreman of the Deluge, and various other toasts.

The hall was impressive, the building having cost $1,800. At the time it was officially opened, it had not yet been completely paid for, however, with aid promised by the city, a speaker stated and, with "the augmentation of their numbers (bringing with them their dues), now reasonably to be anticipated... (the Deluge) would discharge all their responsibilities by next fall."

In Chief Engineer John Keenan's Annual Report to the Governor in 1865, he cites this hall as housing the Deluge Hunneman, the Victoria-built hose cart, a second-class hose cart — undoubtedly the one purchased along with the engine in 1858 — and 750 feet of hose.[17] A bell, used to summon the firefighters and purchased by J. Drummond, the company's foreman, was placed in the cupola. With only 42 members at this time, the Deluge company was more than 20 under strength.

However, by 1877, after only 14 years in these quarters, it became clear that the Deluge hall was no longer adequate, and a new hall was constructed on Yates Street east of Broad. According to the *Colonist* it was an imposing structure

...which is the handsomest in Victoria, occupies a lot 30 by 60 feet; it is a two storey building with a tower, the top of the flagstaff being 100 feet from the ground. The engine house is 27 feet by 48 feet with a yard of 10 feet by 30 feet, the room upstairs will be used by the company for the regular meetings.

As was typical of the period, there was an appropriate ceremonial aspect to the opening. The October 31, 1877 edition of the *Colonist* described the event.

...about 3:30 Hayne's band struck up and the various companies mingled together in a truly fraternal spirit, took the hose carts in tow, then the old hand engine, propelled by the Hook and Ladder men, followed by another hose cart,

[17] Keenan Report, (PABC/C.O./F860-4)

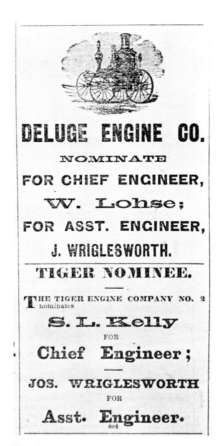

Fire Department elections in the 1870s for officers were duly advertised in the *Colonist*.

and that again by the Tigers dragging the steam engine.... Mr. Spencer photographed the group from the top of Nesbitt's bakery.

The apparatus having been drawn into the house, all adjourned to the room over the engine room which was provided with tables to seat 150 guests and spread by the Levy Bros. with cold chicken, ham and tongue, cold meats of every description, salads etc., and a plentiful supply of liquor.

The Tigers were still in their original quarters at the time of Keenan's 1865 report. The building was still available since this company was the only one renting its quarters. It was providing accommodation for the Tigers' Button and Blake hand engine, its new hose cart acquired at the same time as the one used by Deluge, and 750 feet of hose. Unlike the engine houses of the Deluge and the Union Hook and Ladder, the Tigers' house was not specially designed to house apparatus and so eventually had to be replaced.

In late October 1874, the Tiger Co. house, located roughly on the present-day site of the Royal Olympic Hotel, had a bell tower attached. The fire company bell was imported from England for a total cost of $750.[18] The Tigers were not destined to use it for long because, six years later, in 1880, the company moved into a new wing built onto the southwest corner of the City Hall. The *Colonist* of June 2, 1880, issued a progress report stating that

the structure is rapidly approaching completion and will be ready for occupation early in November. On Saturday last, the Company's bell was successfully lowered from the tower of the house situate [*sic*] on Johnson Street and conveyed to the new building where it awaits elevation. Should a fire occur in the interim the clanging of the deep-toned tongue will not be heard.

The bell, which weighed 1,500 pounds, was hoisted into the tower in the new house in late October and the alarm tested. Many were disappointed that the bell seemed to have lost its normally deep-throated sound, largely no doubt because it was closely surrounded by timbers. However, it was still easily heard at some distance.

The old Tiger house was finally pulled down eight years later, the *Colonist* reporting that "the entire structure, with the exception of the tower, being pulled down bodily, and fully into the ravine with a crash. The tower (for which the Company paid $250) will come down, and thus will disappear another of the old landmarks of Victoria."[19]

The Union Hook and Ladder House which had been built on Hudson's Bay Company land was in an awkward position. The City's centre of gravity had changed, expanding eastward away from the harbour. The location of the hall became increasingly inconvenient for the firefighters, adding unnecessary distance and increasing the time it took to respond to an alarm. By 1870, the building had been relocated to between Fort and Broughton on Government, a move intended to solve this problem. The house was ultimately torn down in the mid-1890s.

The financial burden incurred by the volunteers as a result of keeping pace with advances in technology was considerable. Steam pumpers, while they decreased manpower requirements, and increased efficiency and capacity, cost more to acquire, house and maintain. In order that they could be maintained and operated properly, they required trained

[18] "Large Bell," *Daily Standard*, 5 September 1873, p. 3. The fire bell was ordered from England in anticipation of the tower being completed.

[19] "Another Old Land Mark Gone," *Colonist*, 15 June 1888, p. 3.

staff which, in view of their higher qualifications and licencing requirements, eventually demanded and received compensation for their services.

The added responsibilities of fire department officers led to their being paid for their services. The chief engineer who had overall responsibility for the department, but was not doing the job on a full-time basis, was being paid $700 a year by 1882. Three other officers also received a part-time salary: the Assistant Chief, $300; the Secretary of the Board of Delegates, $300; while the Steward, who looked after the fire halls and horses, was full-time, but at a lower rate of pay than the others at $900.[20]

It had become increasingly clear by 1879 that, for a variety of reasons, the volunteer department was on the way out after more than two decades. The City of Victoria finally and reluctantly assumed full responsibility for the department on New Year's Day, 1886. "Hirelings" replaced volunteers in Victoria as had been the case in many American cities years earlier. An era had come to a close for British Columbia's first firefighters.

C. J. Phillips was the first Chief of Victoria's paid Fire Department in 1886. The helmet was presented to him by a British insurance company.

PABC 4575

[20] R. J. Williams, *British Columbia Directory*, 1882, p. 89.

Chapter 3

"HIRELINGS!": THE OPENING WEDGE

By 1886, protecting Victoria was a vastly greater task for the fire department than it had been less than 30 years earlier. The city had grown to a population of around 15,000 and it occupied an area of approximately 4,500 acres. There were a greater number of high-value brick buildings in the central core and these were gradually replacing the earlier, smaller, wooden structures. Moreover, the city was spreading to outlying districts with the expansion of the road system. The completion of the Canadian Pacific Railway across Canada the year before, and of the Esquimalt and Nanaimo Railway in 1886, made it much easier to travel both on the Island, and on the mainland to points in Eastern Canada — at least in the summer months when the mountain passes were free of snow. Victoria was acquiring some of the sophistication of larger centres; electric street lighting and the telephone had been introduced a few years earlier. In the 1890s, the city would have one of Canada's earliest electric street railways. With all of these changes, the Victoria Fire Department had to change as well.

When the City of Victoria officially took over the department in January of 1886, a three-member Board of Fire Wardens was appointed from among the City Council and was made responsible for all matters relating to fire protection in the city. Among the new Board's first acts was to hire a number of full-time professional firefighters as well as part-time "callmen" to replace the volunteers. By March 1886, the wardens had drawn up and put into force the rules and regulations governing the operation of the department.[1] The hiring of the "callmen" was a "cost-saving" measure and theoretically at least brought the department up to strength. These men were paid, but only when they were called to assist the full-time crews. This was a frequent occurrence, because the department was chronically undermanned. As is so often the case with attempts to save money, this too ultimately proved to be false economy because often the callmen could not be located quickly when required and the delay when they did respond, on occasion made them all but worthless. The system was a bad one, and though it worked after a fashion for a few years, it was discontinued after 1905. It could be argued, however, that the wardens were justified in trying it given that purse strings were tight.

In addition to satisfying manning requirements, the Board had to "take stock" of the situation, generally identifying inadequacies in staffing and halls, and listing the deficiencies found in the apparatus inherited from

[1] *Rules and Regulations of the Victoria Paid Fire Department Adopted 1st March 1886.* Victoria, Cohen, 1886.

the volunteers. On the basis of their findings, they made recommendations for improvements and included these in their first annual report tabled in January 1887. There were three halls in operation at this time — the Deluge house on Yates, the Tigers' situated in a wing of the city hall on Pandora, and the Union Hook and Ladder's, on Government at Broughton. The Hook and Ladder's hall had been moved from Bastion Street some years earlier. In general, it was found that Victoria halls were no longer adequate, being too few in number and, like their apparatus, virtually obsolescent, or becoming increasingly so. Renovations to existing halls would be no more than a temporary measure.

Developments in fire hall design introduced elsewhere in the late 1870s and early 1880s, mainly in the United States, had to be adopted in Victoria as well if fire protection was to be as up-to-date as possible. Such changes as sliding poles, engine heaters, swing harness and improved interior layout dramatically reduced response time and improved efficiency. The Fire Wardens were aware of these innovations and so ordered some upgrading of Victoria halls.

The Deluge hall on Yates Street was enlarged to provide for the horses and, by 1889, a "sliding bar," which "enabled men to reach the ground floor without loss of time" and a heater for the steam pumper, had been installed.[2] While adoption of these improvements did materially improve systems at this hall, it was obvious that this solution was still, at best, a small-scale and short-term one. New and larger halls incorporating modern ideas and technology were essential.

It was not until just before the turn of the century that construction of new fire halls at last got underway in Victoria. This process of renewal was begun with the building of the city's first fully up-to-date "outside" (other than headquarters) hall. It was vastly different from the halls built for the volunteers earlier and so describing it in some detail will give a better idea of the improvements introduced.

One of the areas of Victoria most urgently needing protection was the upper end of Yates Street, some seven blocks east of city centre. Considerable residential development had recently taken place and there was only very rudimentary fire protection in the form of volunteers at the Central School. While the students were trained after a fashion, this was clearly not a realistic solution to the problem. Even energetic teenagers could not be expected to perform as effectively as trained adults.

Nevertheless, hose reels and ladders had been provided on the school grounds for the use of the students should a fire break out in the building. It was hoped that no matter how inadequate, the students could serve as a stop-gap until the fire department arrived from city centre. But what would happen if a fire occurred away from the school itself? Could the residents situated some distance from the school assume that they would receive the help needed — even if the students proved capable. It was indeed a dangerous situation.

The fire chiefs, as early as 1890, had agreed with the residents, feeling that it was impossible to adequately protect the expanding residential districts away from the centre of the city from No. 1 Hall. New halls in a number of outlying wards were needed desperately. Ladders were stored ready for use by anyone in the immediate vicinity of a fire in a number of

2 "Fire Warden's Annual Report" (Dated 4 June 1890) in *Corporation of the City of Victoria Annual Reports 1889*, p. 49.

strategic locations around the city. There is no record as to how their locations were identified.

It took nine years of discussions for residents to convince the City Council that professional firefighters permanently stationed there were needed. The March 26, 1899, issue of the *Colonist* however, announced that at last the long hoped for new fire hall was to be built at the corner of Yates and Camosun streets. Construction began just a day later on March 27, 1899, under the able supervision of the city building inspector. A practical man, he felt that it was desirable to work as quickly as possible to take advantage of the beautiful weather. Only four months later, on July 21, the same newspaper was able to report that work on the hall was almost complete.

... the building is of brick, two storeys in height, and is a modern fire hall in every respect. A tower surmounts the southeast corner of the structure, from which the oldest bell in the province will sound alarms of fire.

The double doors will open on Yates Street, and the horses will stand on either side of the apparatus. The twenty windows throughout the hall afford light during the day while electricity will be used for lighting purposes at night.

The upper storey will be used for sleeping apartments, with a bathroom adjoining. The roof is covered with slate, and a balcony extends over the front doors.

Standing ten feet from the line of sidewalks, and occupying a prominent position on the hill, it is expected that quick time will be made in every direction.

The siting of a fire hall had to be carefully considered, and it was every bit as important a factor as its location within the district. Standard practice in Victoria, as elsewhere during the horse era, was to build fire halls whenever possible on ground higher than the area they were to protect. The reason was simple: if a team of horses had to begin its run to a fire towing heavy apparatus uphill, the animals tired very quickly — obviously a serious problem in a situation where speed was essential. Horse-drawn apparatus in any case had a very short range of probably one to one and one half miles when the team ran at a full gallop. The short range of horse-drawn apparatus made it necessary to have a large number of halls in order to decrease distances between the halls and points within the areas protected.

The apparatus floor of No. 2 Hall, like other Victoria halls built later, was designed to accommodate the horses and reduce response time. The horses' stalls were situated beside the apparatus (in some halls it was behind) and these were equipped with doors that were opened automatically when an alarm came in. The Gamewell system which made this possible, was a major development in reducing response time. It was first used in the United States in a rudimentary form in 1854, and having been in widespread use since then, had been greatly improved by the time it was introduced in Victoria in 1890.

The Gamewell system was an efficient one and greatly shortened reporting time by having call boxes distributed throughout the city at strategic points such as major intersections. Each was connected with the alarm room at the central hall by wires strung on telephone poles in the early days or later, buried underground. As the city expanded to include a greater area, the alarm system was also enlarged in its coverage. The

Electrically-operated fire hall gongs could be heard at some distance. They were an integral part of the Gamewell alarm system.

Looking northwest, Yates Street in foreground, in the late 1880s. City Hall is in centre right.   BCPM

Left:
Possibly the first photo of a Victoria fire. Identified simply as a fire in Chinatown, it may have taken place in 1883. Note the leather hose.   BCPM

The Royal Navy was an essential element of Victoria. These seamen are part of a "sham battle" at Beacon Hill Park in the 1880s.   BCPM

On May 26, 1896, the Point Ellice Bridge collapsed sending an overcrowded streetcar and its passengers into the harbour. Fire Chief Deasy directed rescue operations.   BCPM

Yates, Johnson, and Pandora Streets in the early 1890s, showing the newly-completed Pandora Methodist church.   BCPM

Arches were a popular way of commemorating important events, and this one celebrates the completion of the Esquimalt and Nanaimo Railway in 1886. The Tigers' Johnson Street fire hall can be seen through the arch.   BCPM

Chas. Bush, Engineer of the Deluge. He passed judgement on new apparatus acquired by the Department during the 1880s.   VFD

Having just returned from the great Seattle fire in 1889, these firefighters posed beside the Pandora Ave. Hall. Note the English pattern helmets and belts with small axes. This is the only known instance where these have been photographed.   VFD

The "mortal remains" of the street railway's powerhouse on Store Street following the August 7, 1892 fire. A more substantial brick structure replaced the razed building.   BCPM

This arch, situated on Yates at Douglas is interesting in that one of its supports is the English ladder escape purchased by the volunteers. The arch itself is advertising a Fireman's Ball.   F. D. H. NELSON

system was battery-operated to guard against a power failure. When the lever in a box was pulled, the box number, identifying the location of the alarm, was punched onto a tape at headquarters. Later, the box number code would also be punched by a register onto a paper tape at all the outside halls. Initially, however, this system sounded the gong in the appropriate hall and also rang the city hall bell which alerted the callmen.

The alarm came in to the outside station from headquarters by phone and the Gamewell register simultaneously to ensure that it was received. The hall gong struck the box number, and then the doors of the horses' stalls were opened. The horses, trained to react to the doors opening, walked to the front of the rig, each animal having its accustomed place. The harness for what was usually a two-horse team was permanently attached to the rig, and the head end was suspended from the ceiling by leather straps. This "quick release" or "swing" harness — the terms seem to have been used interchangeably — was dropped onto the backs of the horses by pulling a lever. Collars, split at the bottom and hinged at the top, snapped shut as they fell into place, securing the team to its rig.

This procedure was practised frequently as part of the daily routine; it became second nature to the team. Even when the animals were considered to be fully-trained, the drill was practised often. The gong would be rung and the horses led through the motions repeatedly. Intelligent animals that could be trained readily were a critical requirement for fire departments.

On occasion, however, things could work a little too smoothly and the horses and their apparatus would be on their way before the crew could board them. With the main doors of the hall also being opened by the Gamewell system as the gong struck, there was nothing to prevent the horses leaving. Although it was not a serious problem when practising — the horses would simply round the block and return — it certainly was embarrassing. The hall doors were left open on hot summer days, and a chain would be stretched across the opening to prevent the horses from wandering out. They were allowed to walk around on the apparatus floor where it was much cooler than in the confined space of the stalls.

Returning to the hall from a run, the crew backed the rig in under the leather straps. They then released the team and reattached the harness to the straps, hoisting it to the ceiling once again in preparation for the next alarm. In some halls that later had their original wood-block flooring replaced by concrete, a raised scrub-board pattern was cast into the surface which enabled the quick and accurate positioning of the rig under the harness.

The living quarters above the apparatus floor were equipped with kitchen facilities, dormitory, office, and recreation space, and access to them was usually by stairs from the rear to one side. When a call came in, a sliding pole was used to get to the apparatus floor from the quarters because the stairs took too long. Further time was saved by keeping the turnout gear (helmets, coats, and boots) either adjacent to, or on, the apparatus. The *Colonist* described the apparatus to be used in No. 2.

The combined chemical and hose wagon [to be named the *P. C. McGregor*] will comprise a small fire department in its own right. The one large copper tank will carry sixty gallons of fluid with one hundred feet of rubber hose attached.

Fire Alarm System.

3—Birdcage Walk and Superior St. James Bay
4—Carr and Simcoe Streets   "
5—Michigan and Menzies Streets   "
6—Menzies and Niagara Streets   "
7—Montreal and Kingston Streets   "
8—Montreal and Simcoe Streets   "
9—Dallas Road and Simcoe Street   "
14—Vancouver and Burdette Streets
15—Douglas and Humboldt Streets
16—Humboldt and Rupert Streets
21—Yates and Broad Streets
23—Fort and Government Streets
24—Yates and Wharf Streets
25—Johnson and Government Streets
26—Douglas Street between Fort and View
27—Headquarters Fire Dept. Cormorant Street
31—View and Blanchard Streets
32—Fort and Quadra Streets
34—Yates and Cook Streets.
35—Cadboro Bay Road and Stanley Avenue.
36—Junction Oak Bay and Cadboro Bay Roads
37—Cadboro Bay and Richmond Roads.
41—Quadra and Pandora Streets.
42—Chatham and Blanchard Streets.
43—Caledonia and Cook Streets.
45—Spring Ridge.
46—North Chatham Street and Stanley Ave.
51—Douglas and Discovery Streets.
52—Government and Princess Streets.
53—King's Road and Second Street.
54—Fountain, Douglas Street and Hillside.
56—Oaklands Fire Hall.
61—Cormorant and Store Streets.
62—Discovery and Store Streets.
63—John and Bridge Streets.
64—Catherine Street, Victoria West.
65—Springfield Ave. and Esquimalt Road.
72—Douglas Street and Burnside Road.
123-Avalon Road and Phoenix Place.

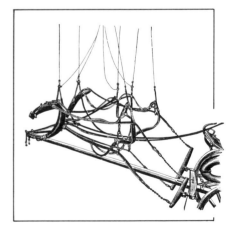

The swing or quick release harness, despite its complicated appearance, was simple and worked well.

In the bed of the wagon will be stored several hundred feet of standard fire hose. While on the sides, two ladders will be carried, with axes, crowbars, and a device introduced by the chief for stretching hose, either from a fire to the hydrant, or from the hydrant in any direction, thereby saving time—one of the principal factors at a fire.[3]

Chemical engines were to prove one of the most effective pieces of apparatus of the era, and the Victoria Fire Department had acquired its first some seven years before No. 2 Hall was even built. Like those elsewhere, the department wholeheartedly endorsed the use of chemical apparatus and their first attempt to acquire such a rig was made in 1890. Babcock hand-held chemical extinguishers, which worked on the same principle, had been used since 1873 and one fire was put out using only Babcocks on July 31, that year. Possibly because they were among the first in the field, the name "Babcock" was soon taken in most departments to mean any hand extinguisher. In his annual report to the city in 1890, Chief Thomas Deasy, who had succeeded Chief C. J. Phillips in 1889, put forward the virtues of the larger chemical apparatus succinctly: "The great advantage in its use is promptness in extinguishing incipient fires. It can be placed in front of a high building with everything ready to go to work, and no danger of damaging goods on the lower floors."[4]

The tank or tanks of a chemical engine contained a bicarbonate of soda solution. By pulling a pin upon arrival at a fire, and then turning a wheel at the end of the tank, sulphuric acid was tipped into the solution. A reaction took place which produced carbon dioxide gas, which expanding, acted as a propellant and forced water out of the tanks to the booster reel and then out through the rubberized hose. Chemical apparatus could be brought into service in as little time as it took to run out the hose from the booster reel. This was much faster than a steam pumper which could take up to eight minutes to get up to working pressure.

A chemical rig was useful in containing small fires quickly, with minimal amounts of water. This was an important consideration in some parts of town particularly. On occasion, districts developed so rapidly that the water mains could not be extended quickly enough to keep pace. Steam pumpers, which needed large amounts of water at a good pressure, could not be used under these circumstances and so, the only way fire protection could be provided was by means of chemical apparatus. In many instances where the mains could handle the steamers, the chemical was still used first because of its greater speed.

While obviously very useful, these chemical rigs could not contain larger fires by themselves—their capacity at best was 100 gallons of water—and they could be dangerous if not operated correctly. If the tank was not permitted to empty completely, or if the valves remained closed after the reaction started, pressure could build and an explosion could result. This applied equally to hand extinguishers, and an incident involving the latter occurred in Victoria several years later in September 1918. The *Colonist* carried an account.

While attending a grass fire on Tolmie avenue last night, Lieut. Joe Lund was killed and Fireman Fred Oliver injured by the explosion of a chemical fire extinguisher which they were using on the fire at the time.

The extinguisher was filled with sulphuric acid and bicarbonate of soda and the

[3] *Colonist*, 21 July 1899, p. 3.

[4] "Fire Warden's Annual Report" 1889, p. 53.

forming of carbonic acid gas is believed to have generated such pressure that the container exploded, smashing Lund's ribs and puncturing his lungs, causing internal hemmorhage The injured man became unconscious soon after he was hurt, and died a short time later. The deputy chief worked over him for three quarters of an hour with a pulmotor, but his efforts were unavailing. The deputy chief at the time of the accident was only ten feet away and was well splashed by the extinguisher's contents. Oliver was not seriously injured.[5]

Probably the delivery hose had become plugged, pressure built and there was an explosion. In the 1890s, despite the possibility of this happening, chemical apparatus seemed to be the answer to a number of problems and the department worked hard to get at least one piece of this equipment.

The chief was successful and a Canadian-built chemical rig manufactured by Morrison in Toronto was acquired in 1892. It was tested successfully on July 7. For test purposes, a fire was set deliberately in an old shack once used to house a forge. Only 10 pounds of soda and a gallon of acid were needed to force the water out onto a blaze.[6] It is fortunate that the chemical did work since the old Deluge engine, brought in as a backup, broke its axle on the way to the test. If the chemical had not worked properly, another steam pumper would have had to have been sent to the scene or the fire could have spread.

The early apparatus of this kind, those delivered before 1900, were exclusively chemical engines, but later ones, classed as "double combinations," also carried hose to serve a steam pumper. These rigs could perform either chemical or hose functions equally well. Combinations were both useful and versatile, and most outside single-bay halls which only had one piece of apparatus were at least initially, equipped with this type.

As Victoria grew, so too did the department's responsibilities as the fire limits were extended to include more of the city. Before the department actually increased the scope of its operations volunteer companies were formed by local citizens to provide interim protection. An additional new hall was added in 1899 to protect the developing residential district of Victoria West, across the harbour from city centre. Before this, the district was served by a volunteer company of 20 which kept their hose reels at the Excelsior Brewery from 1896.[7] Undoubtedly this was a desirable location for after-drill entertainment as well. The exact location is somewhat in doubt today, but it may either have been in the vicinity of Catherine Street at Esquimalt Road or closer to the Point Ellice bridge. In any event, the Victoria Fire Department took over responsibility from the volunteers with the building of No. 4 Hall at the corner of Edward and Catherine streets. Residents in some other districts had also become discontented waiting until the city could provide them with protection. Some formed volunteer companies even earlier than those in Vic West.

People in James Bay, situated to the south of the business district formed their own volunteer company in 1883, thirteen years before the one in Vic West. A small hall suitable for housing an old hand engine and hose reels was built on Kingston Street. The James Bay volunteers, initially known as the "Princess Louise Company," replaced firefighters at No. 1 Hall on Pandora when they were called to a fire.[8] Expansion of

[5] *Colonist*, 2 September 1918, p. 1.

[6] "A New Protector: The Chemical Fire Engine Proves Satisfactory." *Times*, 8 July, 1892, p. 3.

[7] *Colonist*, 22 July 1892, p. 3.

[8] "A New Fire Company." *Colonist*, 30 March 1883, p. 3.

fire protection to include this district became increasingly urgent when the new streetcar system was extended to the Outer Wharf in the early 1890s, a move intended to serve the increased shipping of this period. Inevitably this extension of track led to greater urban and residential development in the area. The frequent arrivals and departures of the trans-Pacific liners from the Far East, Australia and New Zealand, and coastal traffic led to increased activity of all kinds in James Bay. The Victoria Fire Department took over the responsibility from the volunteers for protecting the district in the early 1890s, designating the former volunteers' hall as their No. 3.

The Oaklands district towards the eastern portion of the city was another developing suburban area. From the late 1880s, like Vic West and James Bay, it was initially protected by volunteers equipped with hose reels and ladders. The Chief was permitted to provide at least this level of assistance only because this neighbourhood was a long run for horses even from the new Yates Street hall when that was built. The city would not provide professional fire protection until just before World War I, when No. 6 Fernwood Hall was built—the long delay in providing professional fire protection likely being due to the costs involved.

The central business district of Victoria itself had also grown dramatically during the 1880s and 1890s, especially in terms of the number, value and size of its buildings. It was recognized that downtown fire protection would have to be improved as well and so a new Headquarters Hall was incorporated into the Public Market building in 1899. This magnificent new facility replaced the hall built onto the southwest corner of the city hall for the Tigers in 1880. This hall had also been used by the city-controlled department from 1886. The *Colonist*, on May 16, 1899, included this description of the new Market Building hall:

Chief Deasy and his brigade are now installed in their new quarters, which adapts itself very well to the purposes to which it has at last been put. The fitting up of the barracks approaches completion, and even now the Central station has begun to assume a metropolitan air. The apparatus room is arranged on the principle adopted in New York, Chicago and San Francisco, the various firefighting machines being arranged in two ranks, with the horses behind....

An alarm coming in automatically registers as well as sounding the box, turns on all the lights, and releases the doors of the first rank of horses, which dash to the front and under the harness of the Grant [The 1889 Merryweather steamer], the hose carriage and the chemical. As these go through the main doors their opening releases the second lot of horses for the remainder of the apparatus.

The apparatus room is 50 feet wide by 70 feet in length or 50 x 120, including the stalls behind. The flooring is 3 x 6 planks laid on edge, cemented with hot tar: some idea of its solidity may be formed when it is known that 1100 pounds, more than half a ton—of nails hold it together. The room is light and airy, modern in its every appointment, and complete with automatic-acting release doors, lighters [for the steam pumpers], harness, etc.

On the floor above, Chief Deasy has his office, and a suite of living rooms, the former connecting with the brigade dormitory, from which open the bedrooms of the engineers, drivers and call men. There are also on this floor a large recording gong, the battery and recreation rooms, and a bathroom with a gas heater....

As well as problems posed by increases in the size of the city and its buildings, there were others that stemmed from the widespread introduc-

The well-decorated Merryweather built steamer "John Grant" shown on Douglas Street in the 1890s. Bryant's, the Fire Department blacksmith, is in the background.   PABC 57232

Horsedrawn hose reels made it possible for the hose to arrive at a fire at the same time as the pumpers. Gas torches were mounted on poles at the rear to provide some light.   VFD

The new provincial legislative buildings provided an excellent position from which to view the James Bay bridge and downtown Victoria in 1897. The Empress Hooel was built on a landfill to the east of the bridge six years later.   BCPM

The "P. C. McGregor," of 1899, a chemical built by Champion. Note the foot-operated warning gong.
VFD

The new No. 1 Hall opened in the Market Building in mid-May 1899. The "John Grant" is on the extreme right and the new Waterous engine the "Charles E. Redfern" is beside it.   VFD

No. 5 Hall, built at Douglas and Dunedin in 1908, was a handsome building. There were others like it all over North America.

Thomas Deasy joined the Union Hook and Ladder Company as a torchboy in the late 1860s. Over the next 20 years he rose through the ranks ultimately being selected the second chief of the paid department.   PABC 73295

This hose wagon was photographed at the No. 3 Kingston Street Hall in 1901. The apparatus was painted red at that time.

Built at the crest of a hill, No. 4 Hall Vic West protected districts west of the Point Ellice Bridge.

PHOTOS, VFD

tion of electricity. Ironically, perhaps, electrical power for lighting and the new street railway, wonders of the nineteenth century in the view of many, made the need for greater fire protection more urgent. Electricity had become much more widely used from the early 1880s and uninsulated transmission wires had spread all over the city. Sparks from the wires which shorted out as they touched in heavy winds, could shower down on unprotected and highly flammable shingle roofs. Chief Deasy commented on this danger in his annual report of December 1891.

During 1891 the Fire Department were called upon to suppress fires caused by electrical wires. The firemen find wires hampering them in their work on all principal streets. The men are always willing to fight fire, but they dislike working among wires.... wires run over house tops and through streets carrying death-dealing currents. At any moment, several fires might be caused by crossed wires, and the small fire department of this city would be almost powerless.[9]

The enactment of more stringent fire codes which called for tin roof coverings, and the introduction of insulated wiring greatly improved the situation. The fire department was to be involved with electricity again in the coming years though more with the means of generating it than with the end product.

The street railway's power house, at the south end of the Rock Bay Bridge which crossed the harbour at the north end of Store Street, caught fire early in the morning of August 7, 1892. The alarm was raised by a stranger running in to the engineer's office shouting: "The station's on fire!" Initially, it was a small blaze that could easily have been handled with a bucket or two of water; however, as will often happen, there were complications. The fire broke out in a room used to wind dynamos. Apparently the doors had been left locked and there were no axes readily available to break them in. The fire spread rapidly and at 1:50 a.m. the fire department was alerted. The *Colonist* appearing later that morning described the events.

There was no difficulty in locating the fire — the sky was already fuddy [*sic*] with the ascending flames which seized upon the dry lumber of the electric company's buildings, and devoured them as if they had been kindling, especially prepared for its food. Though the brigade lost no time in getting to work, five minutes showed that the station with all its expensive machinery was doomed.... The water sizzled and steamed as it struck the hot timbers; but the fire was the master element.

Foot by foot, the firemen were driven up the bridge towards the city; the boys with the Babcocks who were attempting to keep the roof of the detached offices from igniting, being forced to slide down the ladders in hot haste.

Then the bridge caught, but was quickly extinguished, and the crowd pressed backward — backward — unable to face the terrible heat.... The engines in the station had not stopped, and the whirring of the machinery and the hissing of the overheated boilers added not a little to the terror of the moment. The crowd fearing an explosion, fell back quickly but not so the firemen, who, from the chief down, fought valiantly and intelligently.... Then the big smokestack fell with a crash and a shout went up from the excited onlookers, as a veritable pillar of fire rose from the ruins. Sparks flew on the wind, and soon the cry was echoed from a dozen throats: "Another fire on Spring Ridge!"

The fire was extinguished about 3:00 a.m. The power house and its equipment were a total loss but the fire was prevented from spreading to

[9] "Report of the Fire Chief." in Corporation of the City of Victoria Annual Reports 1891, p. 10.

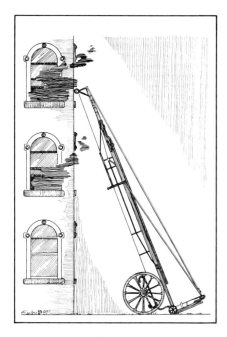

The last piece of apparatus ordered for the volunteer department was a British-built ladder escape. While successful in Britain this type of apparatus was a failure in Victoria.

BRIAN McCANDLESS

residences and other businesses in the immediate vicinity. The Spring Ridge fire, which broke out while firefighters were engaged with the power house, was less serious in terms of the financial loss involved but it did destroy the Civerrtz Brothers' store and a residence. This would not be the end of troubles with electricity for, three years later, the Victoria Electric Tramway and Light Company's power house went up in flames, once again, emphasizing the necessity for better fire protection. The *Colonist* recorded that

...the fire bells rang out at half past twelve yesterday for a fire at the Victoria Electric Light Company's works on Langley Street. Peter Weil had seen the power house was in flames ... when the firemen had arrived the flames seemed to be bursting from all parts of the building. The chemical, the first engine on the ground, quickly got to work and did what it could until four lines of hose were laid, one at the steamer at the corner of Government and Fort streets, and one each from hydrants at Langley and Fort, Wharf and Fort, Langley and Broughton Streets.

Fortunately the building was not very high as the pressure from the hydrants was very weak. . . . The entire inside of the power house was apparently on fire and for a short time, the firemen had hard fighting. To add to their difficulties, there was a barrel of oil blazing close to one of the windows, and when the chemical stream first hit it, the blazing oil spurt [*sic*] out burning foreman Henry of the Chemical in the face, however not seriously.[10]

Furs stored in the adjoining structure, the Boscowitz warehouse, were moved to safety, as there was the very real possibility of the blaze spreading. Fortunately, a supply of coal in the power house did not burn, but the fire loss amounted to $18,000, a substantial amount for the time. Possibly this fire close to the central core of the city had an influence on improving fire protection there as well.

Apparatus

The apparatus situation closely parallelled the development of fire halls when the city took over the department — improvement or replacement were the order of the day. The available apparatus was clearly inadequate and probably quite dangerous, so the city relented and ordered additional new equipment, one piece of which was particularly necessary. A new four-wheeled horse-drawn hose carriage was purchased from the E. B. Preston Company of Chicago in 1888. While horses had towed the heavy steam pumpers for some time, greatly reducing the burden on firefighters, it somehow did not seem inconsistent to continue the hauling of the hose reels by hand. The resulting problem is obvious: the pumpers arrived at the fire quickly, well ahead of the hose which was required to make them fully operational. Having a horse-drawn hose cart rectified the situation.

In the meantime, as the size and height of buildings increased, new apparatus capable of reaching fires effectively had to be acquired. The volunteer department, in an attempt to cope with this problem earlier, had ordered a large two-wheeled English ladder escape from Rose of Manchester in 1885. It was essentially a free-standing aerial ladder which could be wheeled into a confined space in a vertical position. This type of ladder is still carried by British pump/escape appliances, vehicles equipped with both pumps and wheeled escape ladders. While successful in Britain,

10 *Colonist*, 8 February 1895, p. 8.

this apparatus did not work out well in Victoria largely because of the difficulty encountered manoeuvring between power lines, a problem already noted by Chief Deasy.

Fortunately, Daniel Hayes, a San Francisco firefighter had invented a tall extension ladder mounted on a turntable truck in the late 1860s. It was the first true aerial apparatus. Such a rig was valuable because it could put its ladder against any structure without first going through a series of very cumbersome manoueuvres during which it might have fouled power lines. The new aerial could be positioned beside the structure concerned and then the ladder could simply be raised and turned into position. The vehicle also provided a stable base for the ladder.

The *Colonist*, as always, took considerable interest in this new type of apparatus when Victoria's first aerial arrived in December 1889. In its edition of the 20th the paper reported that

...the new truck was duly christened the *William Wilson* in honour of the chairman of the fire wardens...this afternoon an exhibition will be given of the portable extinguisher attached to the truck, at the vacant lot on Government Street opposite the Windsor Hotel.

The new truck is one of the latest production of the Preston Company. It is provided with a seventy foot trussed and back trussed aerial ladder, which is raised by five or six men by means of a right and left hand screw, firmly fastened to the turntable, with two nuts which move horizontally along the screw toward each other, all strain on the screw and nuts being overcome by two sliding bars, which the rollers on the end of the nuts roll on as the ladder is being raised.

The truck is fully equipped, having a fifty foot Bangor ladder [a ground ladder raised against the side of a building using two poles], one thirty foot, one twenty-eight foot, one twenty foot single ladders, and one each sixteen foot and fourteen foot roof ladders, two six gallon fire extinguishers, one Detroit pattern door opener, axes, picks, crow bars, brooms, shovels, forks, wrenches, lanterns, side lamps. The ladder can be used aerially or as a water tower [a nozzle was mounted at the top of the ladder so that water could be showered down upon a blaze] with perfect safety.

The truck is also provided with a permanent steering gear, which turns its back axle and greatly facilitates going to fires by turning sharp curves rapidly. It is provided with a patented tiller lock, by means of which the hind gear can be locked firmly...it can be used without a man in the rear.

Victoria's first aerial ladder truck, named the "William Wilson" is shown alongside the Pandora Fire Hall.

PABC 23607

Victoria's steam pumpers were in extremely poor shape by 1888, with the old Button and Blake machine needing a new boiler and the slightly newer Deluge Merryweather requiring a considerable overhaul. According to the Fire Wardens' report of that year, it was hoped that New Westminster was ready to purchase the Merryweather. Apparently this never took place since there are later references to the engine in Victoria. Even with upgrading—$300 was spent on retubing the engine's boiler in the early 1880s—the Deluge engine was not in first-line condition. Even so, however, it was soon to prove useful in another major fire.[11]

In the first week of June 1889, the 1870 engine along with a hose cart was pressed into emergency service helping Seattle firefighters quell that city's catastrophic blaze. The *Colonist* duly recorded the exploits of the old engine and her volunteer crew.

When the first telegram reached Victoria Thursday, Mayor Grant and Chief of the Fire Department Deasy decided at once to send assistance. The steamer

[11] Retubing of a steam engine's boiler is a part of routine maintenance and is required at set intervals of time, a practice that is necessary from both the standpoint of safety and efficiency. Inspection reports appear in the B.C. Sessional papers as do registrations of boilers.

Potter, which was lying at the Victoria Wharf was chartered at the expense of several gentlemen of that city.... To them [the Victoria firefighters] is due the fact that much wharf property was not destroyed. From the time of their arrival, the engine was stationed on the *City of Seattle* and did not stop working until late last evening [June 8th, 1889]. The Victoria boys were received everywhere with cheers...they gave valuable assistance by extinguishing burning debris along Main Street thus enabling machinist and foundrymen to recover a large amount of valuable iron work.[12]

A total of 22 men, all but four of whom had been members of the old volunteer companies, took the steam Deluge, a hand engine, 1,000 feet of hose and a single hose reel to Seattle. Though they had arrived late — they experienced difficulty in locating Captain Clancy of the *Potter* — they did provide valuable service that was very much appreciated.

In 1889 the situation in Victoria was clearly serious because the old steam pumpers really were not capable of providing the necessary protection on a continuing basis. Fortunately, this problem was understood and a new Merryweather was purchased from the company's agents in Montreal. The engine, ordered from Henry Chapman and Company, was named for Victoria's mayor as was the custom at the time. It was tested and accepted as satisfactory by the Fire Wardens on December 13, 1889, Engineer Bush being well-pleased with the engine. Not only was he pleased, so too were dignitaries and bystanders who adjourned en masse to the Clarence Hotel where copious quantities of liquid refreshment were consumed and toasts to the prosperity of the department drunk.

The new Merryweather and the rebuilt Tiger engine of 1868 were to provide the main fire-fighting "battery" for Victoria over the next decade. Over the years the department would purchase and operate several other steam pumpers, all of which were Canadian-built by the Waterous Company of Brantford, Ontario. The *Charles E. Redfern* was accepted for service on May 5, 1899, another smaller engine of 550 gallons per minute capacity (as opposed to 750 for the *Redfern*) was added in 1909, and two more were purchased in 1911. The *John Grant* was ultimately disposed of in 1917, being almost useless by then.

Steam pumpers were highly effective, particularly when operated in conjunction with a good continuous water supply, but it still took time to raise steam when speed was essential. The earlier machines built before the 1880s could take 8-10 minutes to reach working pressure. The Silsby Company of New York state, a major apparatus manufacturer, along with some other manufacturers, produced a device designed to keep the water in a steamer's boiler at a constant warm temperature while at the hall, thus enabling the engine to build working pressure more quickly. It was an important innovation and one which Victoria, like most departments, adopted. An article appearing in *Appleton's Cyclopaedia of Applied Mechanics*, an excellent contemporary source of detailed descriptions of nineteenth-century technology, described a typical installation:

When standing in the engine-house, a pressure of about ... 5 lbs. per square inch is maintained in the boilers of engines drawn by horses. This pressure is maintained by connecting the boiler of the fire engine with a small, circulating boiler located in the engine-house, the connecting pipes being so arranged that there is a constant circulation of water.

[12] "Back From Seattle." *Colonist*, 9 June 1889, p. 1.

No. 3 Hall Kingston Street was built at the same time as No. 5. The chains across the door openings prevented the horses from wandering off.

The salt water pumping station, equipped with powerful steam pumps, was situated on Telegraph Street. Electrical pumps keep the high pressure system supplied today.   VFD

The apparatus floor of Rossland was essentially similar to most others of the period (1902). Stalls for the horses were situated behind the apparatus. Note the swing harness.   PABC 43730

Right:
Another view of the swing harness, this time at an "outside" hall in Victoria.   VFD

Horses were housed and teamed together throughout their service with the department.

PHOTOS, VFD

The "Boss," Thomas Davis, inspects a "power unit."

Considerable time was spent in training the horses.   VFD

The rebuilt chemical rig was a handsome piece of apparatus in 1909.

Traditionally the Fire Department made a mock run down Government Street as part of the Victoria Day Parade. This run with the Waterous pumper in the lead likely took place in 1911.

In the case of an engine drawn by horses, the circulating boiler is of the simplest description, consisting of a coil of pipe in the firebox of an ordinary coal stove. When the engine is taken from the house, an automatic arrangement shuts the valves connecting the circulating pipes with the boiler of the fire-engine, and opens communication with a tank through which the circulation continues.[13]

A water heater made it unnecessary to have a fire under the boiler while waiting for an alarm—the latter was a risky proposition that had been tried elsewhere. With a water heater, steam pressure could be at a working level within a few minutes of the rig leaving the hall. It both saved time and increased safety. Gas lighters which could get the fire going quickly from a cold start could, and in other locations occasionally did, result in fire if the automatic gas shut-off valve, which became operational as the rig left the hall, did not work properly. Normally in the 1890s—even with water heaters—the fire was not actually started until the engine left the hall. Because of the danger of sparks coming from the steamers' stack setting secondary fires while the rig was en route, some departments did not permit the fire to be started until the pumper actually arrived at the fire location.

The engine itself carried enough water to maintain steam pressure while actually fighting the fire, once again, quoting from *Appleton's*:

Below the Wheelsman's [driver's] seat . . . is a tank, holding about a boiler full of fresh water, from which the supply for feeding the boiler is drawn when salt water is being forced by the pumps and which also furnishes a supply when the engine is proceeding to a fire at a distance. When the engine is drawing water from a hydrant, the boiler feed pumps can also be supplied from the same source.

Simple arrangements are made for choking the springs, in order to prevent vibrations when the pumps are in action. The fuel used for generating steam is cannel coal, which when put into the furnace in large lumps, burns freely and without forming clinker. An engine normally carries sufficient coal for a continuous run of an hour or a little more.[14]

Victoria's steam pumpers were thrown into action on numerous occasions. Even though Victoria was fortunate in avoiding the blazes that almost totally destroyed some cities and towns, there were major conflagrations. In Victoria, they seemed to occur at times when for various reasons the fire department was less able to cope.

In the early afternoon hours of July 23, 1907, a small fire broke out in a lean-to adjoining the boiler house of Albion Iron Works near Fisher's blacksmith shop. The smoke from the fire did not attract attention until it was too late to prevent its spread. The next buildings to go were the old Indian Mission and three other wooden structures. All of these and Fisher's blacksmith shop disappeared in a column of flame which spread sparks over a large area. The summer had been exceptionally dry and the closely packed wood shanties of nearby Chinatown were soon ablaze, sparks being carried by southwesterly winds that seem to blow perpetually in Victoria. The quick response of the fire department did not prevent the lightning quick spread of the fire; even telephone poles disappeared in sheets of flame.

In desperation—their apparatus and water supply were both grossly inadequate—the firefighters tore down five cottages on what is now North Park Street, preventing the further spread of the blaze in that

Heaters kept the water in steam pumpers warm to speed the process of building pressure. Without these devices, it could take eight minutes to reach operating pressure.

[13] Park Benjamin, ed. *Appleton's Cyclopedia of Applied Mechanics*. New York, D. Appleton, 1893. vol. 1, p. 597.

[14] *loc cit.*

The manufacturer was well-pleased with his product in this advertisement.

VFD

direction. The *Colonist* reported that the fire had "blotted out" the block between Store, Chatham, Government and Herald.[15] The only exceptions were four small houses on the south side of Chatham near Store Street. Terrified, people living in the area picked up whatever belongings they could manage and ran for safety.

Thirty soldiers from Fort Macaulay, commanded by Lieutenant Vien, responded to a plea for assistance from Mayor Morley and joined the fight around 4:00 p.m. A half hour earlier the fire had reached the Cavalry Baptist Church at the corner of Douglas and Herald streets, roughly where the Hudson's Bay department store stands now. Attempts to restrict the size of the blaze proved unsuccessful, and when it was over, more than 90 structures had been destroyed and 250 people were left homeless. The fire was to have a major impact on the department. A visiting San Francisco fire official who witnessed the performance of the department and its resources, made some telling comments which highlighted problems, most of which had been created by council's refusal to vote adequate funds for the department.

A number of improvements were put into effect as a consequence of this criticism, the council feeling that they would have to spend some money, build new outside halls and add to the apparatus roster. Two new fire halls were constructed, one at Douglas and Dunedin in the North, and another to replace the old No. 3 on Kingston Street in James Bay. A new salt-water high-pressure system was completed to ensure an adequate water supply and replace the old system of cisterns and regular domestic mains. Steam pumpers could quickly exhaust both these facilities.

Chief Davis was also able to report in early November 1909 that a new three-horse hitch would be added to the big Waterous steamer. This was a practice that was becoming increasingly common elsewhere and had been a recommendation of the San Francisco official. Reducing the load on the horses naturally increased their speed. A new Waterous steam pumper acquired the previous month, was stationed at the headquarters hall. A new hose tower for which the chief had been arguing for some time was nearing completion. It was required both for drying hose and for training.

A new hose wagon to serve the Waterous steamer at headquarters had been ordered from T. M. Brayshaw, a local manufacturer, and was scheduled to be accepted soon. The Brayshaw wagon could carry 50 per cent more hose than the apparatus it replaced — 1,500 feet — and took three months to build, construction being supervised by Chief Thomas Davis. When it entered service on December 9, 1909, the *Colonist* felt the new piece of apparatus sufficiently important to describe it, an unusual situation since hose wagons seldom attracted much notice.

Shining with fresh paint and varnish, beautifully finished and built according to the most modern ideas suggested by long experience . . . it will go out on the next alarm . . . its appearance reflects great credit on the local builder in that it is the equal if not the superior of eastern-built fire wagons. The wheels alone were not built here. They were constructed by specialists at Lawrence, Mass. They are roller bearing and cost in themselves $200.

Davis was quoted in the *Colonist* on the 15th as being pleased with a new service truck that had recently been received from Seagrave in Brockville, Ontario. It was certainly worth the $2,900 it cost. Unlike most

[15] "Victoria is Visited by the Worst Fire in City's History." *Colonist*, 24 July 1907, p. 1.

pieces of apparatus which would, except in unusual circumstances, only respond in certain districts, the service truck was to be sent to fires in any part of the city. It carried equipment that would be useful at almost any fire, but especially those that involved rescue work. Rather than being caught without necessary tools, it was best to simply send out the service truck every time.

By 1909, the Gamewell Alarm system was obsolescent and the department introduced, with the aid of the manufacturer, some improvements. Chief Thomas Davis, who had assumed command of the department in May 1909, following the resignation of Thomas Watson, described some of the problems experienced with the system. In his first annual report of January 1910, he commented that

...the entire system, consisting of gongs, tower bell, door trips and boxes, was operated on a single series circuit, necessitating the use of high battery power and resulting in erratic working, particularly during the wet season when the general leaking was sufficient at times to render the apparatus inoperative.[16]

The answer was to improve the system, providing several circuits rather than a single one. Each outside hall now had its own circuit, but an alarm on one circuit was repeated throughout the system. A new switchboard with six circuits — one for each hall — was also introduced at this time and the wires for the Gamewell system were separated from others in order to prevent shorting out. Overall, there would be less chance of failure in the system, and Victoria was soon to need it.

The David Spencer Fire, 1910

While the city was very fortunate in not experiencing a large number of catastrophic blazes, the one in July 1907 was followed by another more serious fire just over three years later. The fire began in the late evening hours of October 26, its origin apparently being a centre aisle of the David Spencer department store on Government between Fort and View streets. The *Colonist* carried a lengthy description.

C. F. Hine, of the Army and Navy Cigar Store, was leaving the shop at 10:45 when he noticed a small blaze on the ground floor, in the centre of the main aisle, [of Spencer's] seemingly on one of the counters. A moment later one of the two watchmen rushed from the front door shouting "Fire! Fire! Call the firemen!" Mr. Hine ran back to his shop and telephoned for the Fire Department, others seemingly being engaged in telephoning an alarm at the same time. The watchman ran back to try and beat out the flames until driven out.

The flames spread with a rush, the whole inside of the building being aflame when Mr. Hine left his shop, and being alarmed for the safety of his wife and child who were in his rooms in the Five Sisters' block, he ran to awake them and save what he could of his belongings. He ran from door to door waking those residents who had retired and all went to places of safety...

The department arrived in less than one minute after the alarm went in, and Chief Davis, who was not at the hall was brought at the rate of 60 miles an hour to the scene of the blaze.... Arriving at the scene, Chief Davis was among the first to enter the building, and for many minutes later his voice rung the air with his quick, cool-witted orders.

The progress of the fire, highly spectacular in its every incident, was of an

[16] "Report of the Fire Chief." in *Corporation of the City of Victoria Annual Reports 1909*, p. 113.

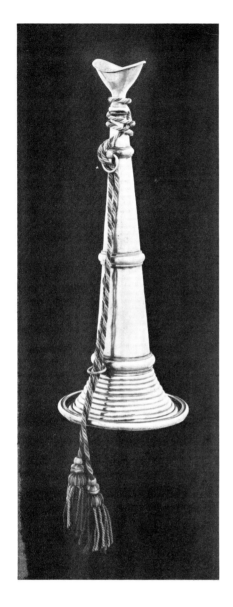

appalling character. The spread of the fire was remarkable for the fact that the wind carried the flames along the top storeys of the buildings. It was apparently impossible for the firefighters to locate the best point of vantage on which to concentrate the streams of water.

By 11 o'clock it was apparent that the building occupied by David Spencer Ltd. was doomed. The entire structure was a seething mass of flames. Whirling showers of sparks and flaming debris were borne by the wind in a southerly direction, the thousands of spectators dodging these as they fell littering the street.

Eating their way into the surrounding buildings, the flames had evidently spread on all sides of the block before it was possible to ascertain where they were to lay their next hold. Spurting across Broad Street, they licked their way through the windows of the Driard Hotel, which time and time again was on fire only to be put out by concerted efforts of three hoses, which for a long time had to be directed from one side of the street to the other. At the Government side the wind swept the fire across the street, and only continuous playing of hose on the buildings lying between Fort Street and Bastion saved the buildings in that area.

Hundreds of the public, who up to this time had been mere spectators of the conflagration, now lent willing assistance in the efforts to prevent the fire reaching further than the block. Ready hands hauled hose from point to point, but any systematic attempts to quell the outbreak were useless.

Across the street, the heat was so great that it broke the plate glass windows of nearly all the stores opposite the block. The owners of the premises within some distance of the fire busied themselves in removing as much of their wares and effects as they could carry, and Bastion, lower Fort Street, Yates Street, Trounce Avenue were piled here and there with office furniture and all manner of goods.[17]

The fire was devastating, with losses totalling approximately $1.5 million and the destruction of an entire city block. Forty businesses were wiped out and several individuals and families who lived in the Five Sisters' block lost everything. It was a terrible experience which, as is so often the case, would have been much worse without the courage and skill of the fire department.

Are you a Teamster?

In the 1980s, it is all too easy to forget what it was like for those working and living around the turn-of-the-century, a period vastly different from our own, especially in terms of the technology. One of the best ways of understanding it, is to relate the experience of individuals who were very much part of it. Hugh Lynn, a native of Belfast and member of the Victoria Fire Department from 1912 to 1950, describes from his own experience what it was like.

At the house where I was boarding, a gentleman suggested that knowing a lot about horses, why didn't I go down to the fire department and see if I could get on. I said, "That's a good idea!" So I went to see the chief [Thomas Davis] and he told me to come back on Saturday morning.

He said, "Are you a teamster?" and I said, "One of the best." Just as he told me a job was available, an alarm came in—the Lemon Gonnason mill on Government Street was on fire. When I returned later, the chief had tears in his eyes. He said that they'd had a very sad morning.

The service truck, while turning from Government Street onto Mill Street, had caught its wheels in the streetcar tracks which swung the pole [the draught bar] around. It struck a telegraph pole and it broke the horses backs, killing them.

Large steam pumpers like this Waterous engine, the "Lewis Hall" were very heavy and so teams were increased to three horses. The canvas behind the front wheels protected the pump mechanism from mud and dirt. Victoria had four Waterous steam pumpers in service by 1911.

The fire department was like a large family.

Recreation was part of the routine and "Old Maid," a standard test of skill.   PHOTOS VFD

H. P. McDowell. Victoria Fire Department uniforms were almost identical to those worn elsewhere in North America.

Chief Watson's quarters at No. 1 Hall in 1902.

Musical pursuits were popular with Victoria's firefighters.

A fire hall was home to many single Victoria firefighters.   PHOTOS VFD

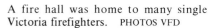

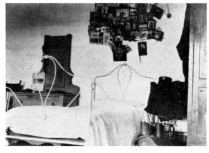

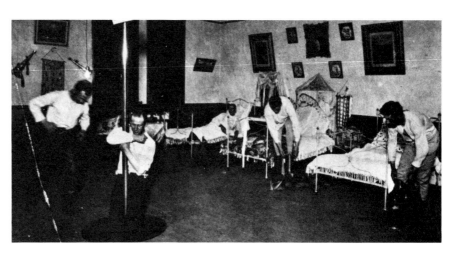

Right:
Quarters were the scene of frantic activity when an alarm came in at night. This is Rossland, but the same scene occurred universally.   PABC 4373

Turnout gear—protective clothing—was just as bulky 80 years ago as it is today, but the materials used were vastly different.

For a number of years Victoria apparatus was painted white with black shadowed gold lettering.

Above and Opposite:
The scale of the July 23, 1907 fire which destroyed several city blocks was terrifying, with the homes of the poor, the rich, the law-abiding and the disreputable suffering the same fate. An attempt was made to move furniture out of these houses, but efforts ceased when the situation became too dangerous.   PHOTOS VFD

Spit and polish are indicative of an efficient, well-disciplined department with a high morale. On the basis of this photo, Victoria qualified on all counts.

After a long service and many rebuilds, the 1870 steam Deluge was relegated to pumping out basements. The original boiler was long gone and the engine was rigged for horses.

Lt. Russell, Hugh Lynn, and Joe Hopkins, c. 1913.   H. LYNN

The spectacular David Spencer department store fire of October 24, 1910.   VFD

The rebuilt 1892 Chemical was a handsome rig.

Playpipes, Nozzles and Babcock extinguishers, the tools of the trade.

PHOTOS, VFD

The aftermath of the Spencer fire. The Arcade building later constructed on this site also suffered a serious fire in the 1920s.

"Do you still want to drive for the fire department?" I said, "You can't keep a good man down."

Lynn was instructed to report to No. 5 Hall the following Monday morning for his driving test on the American LaFrance Hose Chemical that had gone into service in 1909. The test was simply to determine if he was as good as he claimed to be. In fact, though his experience riding horses was extensive, he had never driven a team before!

So I went back on Monday, Labour Day 1912, and as I arrived, an alarm came in. I watched the rig go out. Later on, I walked back and had a look at the horses and thought, Lynn, you've made a big mistake this time!

Anyhow, I've never put in a more miserable night in my life. So that night, I never slept a wink. The next morning, Deputy Chief [Vernon] Stewart came out and took me for a drive as far as Washington Avenue on Burnside. "You're a damn good teamster!" he said, just like that. He said "I've tried men out and they haven't done as good a job with the horses!" Anyhow, I came back happy and satisfied.

Having proven himself capable, and moreover, having a knack for caring for horses — he had grown up around horses in Ireland — Lynn was to provide the care for the horses at any hall to which he was assigned. Then as now, men were transferred between various halls both for purposes of relieving other men, and so that they could familiarize themselves with the different districts and the varying problems they could present.

The horses used by the department were always strong, fast, and intelligent — carefully chosen for their job. In Victoria as elsewhere, they were given short masculine names ("Togo," "Tom," "Jack," "Duke," "Prince," "Bob," etc.) for the sake of simplicity in what could often be confusing circumstances. They were well-trained and came to respond quickly. Lynn remembers:

If the telephone went when the horses were eating, they would stop and cock their ears. If there was any commotion such as the sound of running feet, some would break out in sweat — I've seen horses leave the hall with perspiration rolling off. They weren't afraid when you got to a fire and you could leave them as close to fire as you liked. We had a weight we'd tie them to to keep them from running around. I'd leave them attached to the rig, tie them up, put a blanket over them, and go off to fight the fire.

It was a hard life for horses, they didn't get enough exercise. To give them a run, we'd have to stay within the sound of the gong which meant staying within a block or two.

I'd be up at 6:00 a.m. and by 7:00 I'd take them for a run — I'd ride one and lead the other, go around the block a few times and then go for breakfast where I was boarding. After this, I'd come back and start grooming the horses. It would take me all morning and I'd go for lunch.

When I'd got back to work, I'd harness to clean — it got full of hairs. I had all sorts of equipment there for cleaning, but I wouldn't clean the brass, looking after the horses was a 24-hour job.

Working conditions compared with those in other jobs at that time; hours were long and, by today's standards, strict descipline was maintained. Lynn, again:

I worked a 24-hour shift and had one day off a week — Friday. For this, I was getting $64.50 a month, very good wages in those days. If you were leaving town and going on a holiday, you had to tell the chief where you were going. On your day off, if a general alarm came in, every man would be needed and you'd have to respond.

Chief Davis was quite a disciplinarian. If a man was caught smoking outside the hall while in uniform, he'd get a week's holiday without pay. And if you went out there after your work was done, you had to dress up [in uniform] and have a crease in your pants. And Davis, when he left, he said to me, "Lynn, you were always tidy."

When Davis got his first automobile — he was a great man for speed — he wanted to get on the job and beat everyone else. So this one afternoon in the Burnside firehall, there were four of us who were sitting at the back window and, by golly, we saw smoke and flames at the Moore-Whittington mill.

I said to the lieutenant, "Look at this!" and he said "There's a fire!" So we went downstairs, got the horses and wagon and then phoned headquarters, and we were gone. So the alarm went through headquarters, and we were gone and as he [the Chief] came out, he saw this smoke, there was lots of smoke. So when he turned from Garbally and from there turned down David, I beat him around the corner with the horses. When I got off the wagon, he called to me and said, "Lynn, you drive too bloody fast!" So I said, "You're a pretty fast driver yourself, Chief."

Emergency vehicles even during the horse era were driven at high speed, and Deputy Chief Vernon Stewart, right from the outset, explained to Hugh that fire rigs were driven differently. Hugh explains:

Fire horses don't trot, they gallop, and that's why we have these loops on the reins, and when you get into your seat, you fasten your seat belt or the horses will pitch you out of your seat. You get your hands in the loops and when the horses are galloping, you go with them like this (rocking forwards and backwards).

I used to talk to the horses the whole time I was driving — 'Easy boys, easy boys' — they knew the sound of my voice. And when they were coming up to where I had to make a turn, they'd slow up there without having to taut the reins — they knew they were going to slow up.

The brakes on fire apparatus were applied in a different manner from other horse-drawn rigs. A foot-operated bar running across the footboard in front of the driver's seat was used rather than a long lever on the right side. The driver's hands had to be free to control the horses at high speed. The centre-mounted warning gong, used as a siren would be today, was also foot-operated, usually by the officer who normally sat on the left side of the driver's seat. Behind the seat was a whip lash which, according to Hugh, was seldom if ever used. The horses, not wearing blinders, could see if the driver was reaching for it. "As soon as you reached for it," Lynn recalls, "they were gone!"

Usually the horses were easy to handle, but there could be exceptions. One day, Hugh was told that two horses had to go to the blacksmith for shoeing, and because it was a nice day, Hugh decided to ride one and lead the other. He had to go from No. 3 Hall in James Bay to the blacksmith, roughly where Centennial Square is today. Not heeding warnings against taking both animals at the same time, Lynn set off. After travelling a few blocks the horse being led decided to sample a particularly choice bed of grass on a boulevard and broke away from Lynn. Unable to coax him back, Hugh dismounted and inevitably, his horse joined the first. Fortunately, a police constable happened along and both animals were soon rounded up. Once again on their way, everything went well until they reached the Arcade building on Government. In the front window of the restaurant was a lady eating what appeared to be a particularly delicious meal. The first horse, his earlier snack having been interrupted, once again broke ranks and entered the cafe. The meal was consumed — but not by the lady in question.

Things were to change dramatically for firefighters in Victoria over the next few years. Hugh Lynn's beloved horses, like fire horses elsewhere, disappeared in favour of motorized apparatus.

Chapter 4

MOTORIZATION: GOODBYE TO LOYAL FRIENDS

The Victoria Fire Department, like many others, was eager to make the transition to motorized apparatus. As early as 1906 Chief Thomas Watson recommended in his annual report that "a motor auxilary wagon, capable of carrying men, chemical extinguishers, etc., be purchased and placed at headquarters, and a motor engine (pumper) also be purchased." Watson and most of his contemporaries wanted to replace the horses used by their departments as quickly as possible.

While justifiably regarded with great affection horses were expensive and inefficient when compared to the new motor apparatus coming into service in the early 1900s. Unlike the new trucks, horses needed care even when not responding to alarms and they consumed large quantities of expensive fodder regardless of whether or not they were working. If they fell ill, they had to be provided with costly medical care. Considerable space in the fire hall was required to house the animals and the horse-drawn rigs took up more space than their motor equivalents due to their draw bars and harnesses. The very necessary "mucking out" or cleaning the stalls, was not popular with the majority of firefighters. This unpleasant task took considerable time, and often had to be done when the men were tired. Grooming the animals and providing them with adequate exercise were not overly popular jobs, and at most halls these duties were assigned to junior men or those few, like Hugh Lynn, who liked the work. For all these reasons, replacing the horse had long been a major objective with firefighters.

Some of the earliest attempts to replace horses with machines took place in fields other than fire-fighting. There had been a number of experiments with self-propelled steam vehicles in Europe. Some of these, like that of Nicholas Joseph Cugnot in France in the 1760s achieved at least a limited degree of success in that the vehicles were able to move under their own power. Cugnot designed and built a steam-powered tractor which he hoped would replace horses for towing artillery pieces. The experiment worked out as well as could be expected given the primitive nature of the technology, but the vehicle did lack one important feature—brakes. The result was inevitable. There were other attempts at perfecting a self-propelled vehicle, some of which enjoyed a fair degree of success, such as Richard Trevitheck's buses in England. It was not until 1840 that a self-propelled piece of fire apparatus was to appear. When Paul Hodge of New York built a two-ton pumper in that year it was found that the machine worked after a fashion, but it was extremely cumbersome, slow, and all but unmanoeuvrable. Another attempt, equally unsuccessful, at producing a self-propelled steam pumper was made by Joseph Latta nine years later in Cincinnati.

Efforts to perfect the self-propelled steam pumper continued throughout the nineteenth century. The most successful of these attempts seemed to come from the Amoskeag Company, a long-time American manufacturer of more conventional horse-drawn steam pumpers. Amoskeags were among the most widely used self-propelled steam pumpers, at least in North America. Several large city departments, which were determined to replace their horses, invested in these large, extremely cumbersome juggernauts. Even Vancouver, possibly inspired by recollections of the town's destruction by fire in 1886, purchased one of these machines — the engine in fact survived in other hands until the early 1940s when it was scrapped. The English Merryweather Company, too, produced a self-propelled steamer which was tested in October 1899. It proved capable of climbing a steep hill at 10 mph and could hit a scorching 20 mph on the level.[1] So successful were these machines that horse-drawn steamers disappeared from the Merryweather catalogue by 1902. However, the basic problem of size, weight, and consequent poor manoeuverability persisted, and it was readily apparent that a new and more compact power source was needed.

The creation of the first commercially practical gasoline-powered vehicle and the subsequent progressive refinement of the internal combustion engine made the eventual acceptance of self-propelled fire apparatus a foregone conclusion. It was not until almost two decades after its invention in Germany in 1885 by Gottlieb Daimler and Carl Benz that the gasoline engine became a practical alternative to horses in firefighting. Steam was no longer a serious contender from this point. The internal combustion engine, even by the first years of this century, was relatively powerful, light and compact, and potentially at least, reliable.

Both electricity and steam still had their advocates for powering autos and trucks, with companies like Baker espousing the former and White and the Stanleys the latter. Both electric motors and steam engines had range problems, and it became clear before long that gasoline engines were the only realistic answer. Fire departments, like freighting and cartage companies, optimistically looked upon gasoline-powered vehicles as the most practical replacement for horse-drawn rigs. The big problem was to convince the politicians to spend the money for the new apparatus.

In 1903, the year the Wright Brothers first took to the air in their gas-engined airplane, the chief fire officer of Finchley, a suburb of London, England, was inspired to approach the borough council with a view to puchasing a motor pumper. It would, if Chief Sly had his way, not only have a gasoline engine to propel it, but would also be equipped with a pump powered by a gas engine. This was a major innovation since never before had both functions, "petrol" propulsion and pumping, been combined in a single vehicle. To succeed, engines had to be powerful enough to do what was required of them and the very complex gearing that was necessary for self-propulsion and pumping both had to be developed. A Capitaine Cordier of the Paris fire brigade actually succeeded in intro-

[1] David Burgess-Wise. *Fire Engine and Fire-fighters*, London, Octopus, 1977, p. 83.

ducing a gasoline-powered though horse-drawn pumper to his department in July 1899. Horse-drawn gas and electric pumps had the advantage of being much quicker into action than steamers which had to wait to raise steam pressure.

The Finchley borough council at last relented after making some objections, most of which reflected ignorance of the new technology. Merryweather, the same British company that had supplied Victoria with steam pumpers earlier, was able to provide Finchley with a motor pump on an Aster chassis — exactly what Chief Sly wanted. This apparatus was delivered in 1904 and provided excellent service for many years. More significantly, news of its success among other manufacturers and especially firefighters convinced others that gas-engine-driven pumpers were both reliable and desirable. There were, of course, chemicals and ladder trucks that were motor driven as well. The Finchley pumper, still exists in the collection of London's National Science Museum in Kensington.

Four years later Victoria found itself committed to building two new fire halls; No. 3 in James Bay and No. 5 at Douglas and Dunedin in the North Ward of the city. With this expansion of its facilities it was obvious that the department would be looking at new apparatus with which to equip them. With the demonstrable success of British motor engines ("appliances" as they are termed in Britain) it was not unreasonable to expect that Victoria too, should consider purchasing motor apparatus. Chief Thomas Watson had recommended this in his report of September 1907. Thomas Plimley Ltd., a local automobile dealership, announced its proposal to supply Victoria with an English motor apparatus, a chemical engine, in the July 10, 1908, issue of the *Times*. In a Letter to the Editor, Plimley's quite correctly stated that

The majority of fires start from small causes and rapidly increase until, upon arrival of the ordinary fire engine [the horse-drawn steam pumper], they have gained such proportions that the difficulty of subduing flames is very greatly increased. The self-propelled chemical engine is relatively light in weight and can travel at high speeds with safety, the consequence being that it is at the required point with very little loss of time, and can discharge a stream of liquid on the flames before they have gained large proportions. Then again the Chief can find a seat upon the vehicle and this can be the spot to formulate his plans should the conflagration threaten to become a large one.

The engine that we have in mind for the city is a specially built one and constructed to be used over any kind of road . . . the weight is 35 cwt with full equipment, including two folding ladders. The driver's seat is roomy and holds two with ease, while the platform projecting from the back of the chassis will accommodate two passengers. Each of the two tanks has a capacity of 25 gallons and after completion has to undergo a test of 200 lb. to the inch. One tank is discharged at a time.

Neither Plimley's nor Chief Watson's efforts were to prove successful and horse-drawn double combinations, hose/chemicals, were ordered from both American LaFrance and Seagrave for delivery later. Both companies manufactured up-to-date steel-bodied apparatus which were fully-equipped by the standards of the period despite not being motorized. Seagrave apparatus had never been ordered for Victoria in the past and this purchase was essentially an experiment. It is difficult to say for certain why the city council would not purchase the motorized rigs. Most

The criticism that followed the July 1907 fire had the effect of loosening city council's purse strings. The purchase of this steel-bodied combination and other badly-needed apparatus was a result of this criticism.   VFD

The Vancouver Fire Department experimented with steam self-propulsion in 1908 with this cumbersome Amoskeag. Victoria wisely waited for suitable internal combustion power. The Amoskeag survived into the 1940s when it was scrapped.   VCA

This Seagrave is a combination unit. Like its horse-drawn equivalent, it carried hose to serve the steam pumper in addition to its chemical equipment.

Later chemical apparatus had twin booster reels carrying rubber hose. No other hose was carried.

PHOTOS, VFD

"My idea," (said Thomas Davis) "would be to have a two seat machine of a runabout pattern. ...I could reach a fire in the shortest possible time and hold it in check until the arrival of other apparatus..."*Colonist*, December 1909

The service truck and three steamers were motorized with Seagrave Type D tractors in 1912.

This "driver" of Chief Davis's car had some difficulty in reaching the controls.

Chief Davis came to Victoria from Toronto and served until 1918.

PHOTOS VFD

The apparatus at the Victoria Day Parade in 1913 was quite different from that only two years earlier when horses towed the service truck along the route.

On November 11, 1914, a fire broke out in the Hibben Company stationery storage on Government Street. The well-trained fire horses did not panic if left near a fire.   PABC 8721

likely it was their higher purchase price since the council had habitually been reluctant to provide adequate funding. As if to prove this, in 1906 many firefighters were forced to quit their jobs and move elsewhere because of the "meagre" wages, and because uniforms were not provided.[2] In fairness, however, it may also have been due to the council's unfamiliarity with, and therefore distrust, of motor apparatus. There is also the possibility that availability may have been a problem although this seems unlikely because later purchases were also horse-drawn. Quite likely it was a combination of elements.

However, within three years of the ordering of these horse-drawn rigs, the first motor fire apparatus was ordered from Seagrave. Possibly the more widespread acceptance of motorized apparatus had had its effect, but possibly too, events such as the David Spencer fire described earlier may have had an influence. In Victoria, purchases of new apparatus often seemed to occur after major fires. In any event, Seagrave had from 1909 produced fire apparatus powered by a 4-cylinder air-cooled engine, and had undertaken the manufacture of this motorized apparatus in Woodstock, Ontario. The trucks purchased for Victoria (Vancouver had ordered some a year or two earlier and Kamloops and Prince Rupert were also to order this type of rig) were Type AC 53 hp vehicles known affectionately as "Flatfaces" wherever they were used. The contract proposed for a later delivery included detailed specifications for similar vehicles. The chemical was described as having

Two sixty gallon tanks, made from heavy Lake Superior copper sheets, head hammered and handsomely pebbled. Seams and heads rivetted with copper rivets. All seams, joints and parts exposed to chemicals heavily hand tinned to make smooth surface inside to prevent corrosion and leakage. The finished tank is guaranteed to stand a hydrostatic pressure of 250 lbs. to the square inch. All piping, elbows, tees, and valves have one inch opening, joints thoroughly tinned and made with long standard threads. The acid dumping device and agitator paddles are on separate shafts and are operated from the end of tank. The tank is fitted with a 2½″ hose connection and valves whereby the tank may be filled from hydrant or water passed through chemical hose without entering the tank. The chemical hose is coupled with heavy brass couplings from our own patterns, and is tested from the inlet to the tank through the tank connections to the chemical shut off nozzle to 250 lbs. to the square inch.

Fire equipment:

2 pickhead fire department axes
1 crowbar
2 brass fire department lanterns
2 pressure gauges, 400 lbs capacity (fitted)
2 acid bottles for each cylinder, fitted as stated above
2 acid bottle cannisters, fitted as above
1 copper acid measure and funnel
2 chemical nozzles
2 3 gallon hand extinguishers
   all necessary wrenches, etc., for chemical tanks

Chassis Equipment:

1 complete tool kit
1 5 ton quick acting jack
1 search-light equipped with sparking device for lighting

2 "Resigned from Department." *Colonist*, 6 September 1906, p. 10.

1 presto light tank
1 storage battery
1 separate coil for lighting search-light
1 hand siren
1 hand horn
2 oil cans
4 spark plugs
2 spare drive chains[3]

The trucks had air-cooled 4-cylinder gas engines mounted below the driver's seat and hard, solid-rubber tires. Although the British inventor, John Dunlop had produced the first air-filled tire in 1902, one of several developments occurring simultaneously that made motor vehicles both practical and desirable, it was not until the 1920s that both manufacturers and users of trucks trusted pneumatic tires. Most continued to prefer the extremely rough-riding but puncture-proof solid rubber type.

The arrival and subsequent test of Victoria's first motor Seagrave on June 2, 1911, proved popular with a number of Victoria politicians who were taken for a ride—literally though not figuratively. The *Times*, the following day, carried an account of the test which was dutifully written in the typical prose of the day.

What a ride it was! The leviathan sigh of the motor siren heralded the approach of the gigantic vehicles, and as one attempted to see them in their mad career they disappeared like vaporous shadows in a cloud of consumptive-looking dust. For those who participated, it was a never-to-be-forgotten ride. It was without, from start to finish, the sort of thrill that sends blood coursing through the germ soaked channels like water through a sleeve and elicits the consciousness of change to the point where experience outrivals the preservation of life.

The new chemical truck and hose wagon, which were in "the best ivory white with gold trimmings" sped through city streets with the mayor and some councilmen hanging on. When "country" streets were encountered, all the stops were pulled out and high speeds—40 mph—were attained. This demonstration was an astute public relations move on the part of the fire department. The trucks, which were in effect on probation, were immediately afterwards accepted by the mayor and council, and taken on strength by the department. These vehicles were direct replacements for horse-drawn apparatus, being similarly equipped to the horse-drawn rigs, with the exception that the amount of hose or chemicals they carried was significantly greater. They were also much faster and obviously never experienced fatigue.

The "flatfaces" were to see long service in Victoria and were still in front line service when Gray Russell, who was to serve for 40 years, joined the department in February 1926. He recalls that

I drove the "flatfaces". They had acetylene for the lamps—the headlights—and they carried a big tank which was for the soda and acid. That was the chemical for small fires. They were kind of light, all the weight was in the back with the hose. They used to get around pretty good. They didn't go very fast but they were fast enough.

[3] Contract proposal Between the City of Victoria and the W. E. Seagrave Company Dated 18 September 1911, p. 4.

There was a serious problem relating to the use of the solid tires and this was to have tragic consequences in October 1925. One of the old Seagraves skidded on rain-slicked streets and overturned while responding to an alarm. One firefighter was injured slightly when he was thrown clear but another, Fred Medley, was killed.[4] The truck was so badly damaged that it was written off. Joe Norman, the son of Captain Charles Norman, and himself a firefighter in the early 1930s, recalled that in the case of the wood paving block streets in Victoria, ice and solid rubber tires could be a deadly combination, because water would settle between the blocks and freeze resulting in a surface that was too slick to provide traction.

The original Seagrave trucks were soon joined by three additional trucks. A proposal was submitted by Seagrave on September 18, 1911, for supplying 1-Type D 80 hp tractor for the aerial, 1-Type D tractor for the city service ladder truck, 1-Type D 80-hp tractor for the steam fire engine; 1-53 hp Double 60-gallon chemical engine; and 1-43 hp Chief's automobile. The price was $30,000 and the terms were straightforward: CASH.[5] New motorized apparatus was soon acquired; these were built by Seagrave.

Many departments, as well as Victoria, continued to purchase steam pumpers at this time. When first taken on strength by the department the pumpers were towed by horses, but before long they too were motorized. As they had been virtually new when the process of motorization began, replacing them with motor pumps; even if these were readily available, and as yet they were not, would have been wasteful. Motorization was a very expensive and complex process involving new training and even changes to fire halls. In order to save money on apparatus, some departments attached a front-wheel-drive rig directly onto the chassis of the steam pumpers, giving a single, rigid-chassied vehicle. Others added a two-wheeled "tractor" built by Christie or LaFrance, or three-wheeled Knox power units to their steamers. Victoria went a slightly different but even less costly route of simply replacing the horses with a Seagrave 80 hp type D tractor attached to the steamer where the front axle in horse-drawn configuration swivelled.

In his annual report tabled in January 1912, Chief Thomas Davis who had succeeded Thomas Watson three years previously, came out strongly in favour of replacing even more of his horse-drawn apparatus. He could make a much more credible case because by this point the Seagrave motor apparatus had been in service for some months. Davis wrote that the purchase would be justified.

This would not only be a big saving in the cost of maintenance over the present horsedrawn apparatus, as I estimate that by placing these motor apparatus in service a saving of $1,152.00 annually can be saved over the keep of ten horses, which is required to handle these different apparatus, not alone taking into consideration, the increased 50% efficiency that motor apparatus adds to the fire department.

... I may add that since our motor apparatus went into service on June 2nd 1911, up to the present, it has not cost the Department one cent for repairs through any fault of the manufacturer or construction. It must be understood that one of these wagons carries almost double the amount of hose carried by horsedrawn apparatus, the other more than 700 feet more than the wagon it replaced.[6]

The roster of motor rigs was progressively increased with an additional Seagrave Type D 80 hp tractor being ordered on April 10, 1913. Because

[4] "Driver Killed When Speeding Wagon Crashes." *Victoria Daily Times*, 26 October 1925, p. 9.

[5] Contract Proposal by W. E. Seagrave Company to the City of Victoria dated 10 April 1913, p. 2.

[6] "Report of the Chief of the Fire Department (dated 2 January 1912)." in *Corporation of the City of Victoria Annual Reports 1911*, p. 226.

New

Foamite Chemical Equipments for mounting on all types of motor fire apparatus

MANY members of the Pacific Coast Fire Chiefs Association have already found FIREFOAM, applied by FOAMITE Equipment, to be the most effective method known for extinguishing fire of **any kind.** It is the only method that surely controls fires of oil, gasoline, grease, etc.—the quickest-acting and least damaging method to use on any type of fire.

Their trucks carry the FOAMITE "FD" Extinguisher—the modern first-aid weapon adopted by fire chiefs all over the country.

The remarkable success of FOAMITE Protection has created a demand for a larger unit adaptable to any type of motor apparatus. Foamite-Childs engineers have met this demand with the new FOAMITE 40-gallon chemical tank. Above, this equipment is shown installed in place

of the familiar but less effective soda-acid tanks.

When put into action, the chemical solutions in the double tank unit generate about 600 gallons of fire-smothering FIREFOAM. A pressure cylinder mounted on the running board discharges the two solutions separately through a twin hose line, giving the stream of FIREFOAM (mixed fresh in the combination Siamese nozzle set) an effective fire-extinguishing range of about 50 feet from the nozzle.

Any motor apparatus already in service or now being constructed can have this up-to-date FOAMITE fire-fighting equipment. It is furnished in either single tank or double tank units; polished copper or nickel-plate finish, as desired.

Send for detailed information about FOAMITE Motorized Pumpers and other Fire Department Equipment.

Foamite-Childs Corporation
OF CALIFORNIA
FIRE PROTECTION ENGINEERS

[7] The *Russell* was unusual in that it was built in Canada by a subsidiary of the well-known bicycle manufacturer C.C.M. It was powered by an American *Knight* engine, hence the name *Russell-Knight*. In one or two Annual Reports this same vehicle appears to be cited as a *Thomas-Knight*.

the operational range of motorized apparatus was much greater, the number of halls required to protect the city could be reduced. Those parts of the city that they had protected could be covered by motor apparatus from other halls. Included among these, somewhat ironically, were some that had been constructed after the introduction of the first trucks. The unused halls were often rented and then sold. The number of horses on strength also decreased progressively as new motor rigs, such as an extremely modern-looking Nott "worm drive" hose truck taken on strength in 1914, were introduced, and by 1918 all horses had been taken out of fire department service. Victoria was motorized before New York City. That was admittedly a slightly bigger job!

Often, departments that had budget problems, and Victoria inevitably was one, would purchase an automobile or truck chassis and convert it according to their needs instead of ordering expensive custom built rigs like the Seagraves. The conversion was simple, the automobile chassis was lengthened, a "homemade" fire apparatus body attached, and the appropriate equipment added. Victoria followed this route and took a Kissel Kar and a Russell-Knight on strength in 1917 following their conversion.[7] These were the only pieces of apparatus added since the Nott Universal hose wagon in 1914, a vehicle which suffered from losing one of its wheels due to weak axle spindles. There are accounts of wheels shooting through store or restaurant windows as the truck hit the ground. Some aspects of fire-fighting, while not quite this exciting, are still very much part of the story.

Fire Hall Routine

Life around a Victoria fire hall, while obviously not dull when an alarm came in, could settle into a comfortable routine with chores taking up much of the time. Waiting for a call could add to stress and this nervous energy was often dissipated in practical jokes, as Hugh Lynn recalls

There was this chum, Harry Anderson, a big Swede. He was crazy for pulling tricks. Well, we called at 8 o'clock in the morning at headquarters and we'd generally go upstairs for half an hour and gather around a big pot-bellied stove. Merrifield was the Chief's driver and he'd fallen asleep. So Anderson got a little piece of paper and he went over to the stove, opened the door, put the tray down and got some of the ash, the black ash. And he went over to Merrifield and blew it onto his face . . . and what a hell of a mess his face was. And then he [Anderson] went down and put in an alarm, and because he was driving the Chief, Merrifield went to the chief's car. The Chief says to him "Where the hell have you been?" Merrifield says, "I was upstairs." "Go and look in the glass." Merrifield said, "I'll kill those bastards!"

He was not the only victim Harry Anderson was able to catch out and sometimes the jokes would get somewhat bizarre.

There was this chap, Charlie Atkinson, who bred goats. Sometimes we use to put a mouse in his locker tied up by its tail. He'd go to his locker and there would be the mouse, a rat or dead cat. So one day he had a goat that he brought down to sell at the market — he was going to give it to one of the farmers to sell for him. Atkinson went down and couldn't find the chap that was going to sell it, and so the goat was tied up downstairs. So Anderson brought the goat upstairs and put

Lower Yates Street during the great snow of February 1916. After a few days city street crews and the Army dug the city out from under the "white stuff."   PABC 64132

Victoria firefighters did their best to cope. Had a fire occurred — fortunately, it did not — response would have been by sled. But how would they have located and unfrozen the hydrants?

Left:
The big Seagrave aerial was not motorized until 1918. It was used in a film made during World War I.   PHOTOS, VFD

Two passenger cars, a Kissell Kar and a Russell-Knight were converted into fire apparatus during World War I as an economy measure. They were intended to provide motor service to the remaining outside halls.

The drill yard with a Bangor ladder against the rear of No. 1 Hall. The poles were used to raise and then support the ladder. The tower was built in 1918 after years of agitation by chiefs.   PHOTOS VFD

By early 1918, the apparatus at No. 1 Hall was almost completely motorized, but steamers still represented the sole pumping power.

Left:
The chain on the wheel on the right improved steering. Smooth tires had difficulty in maintaining traction. Seldom has so much "ham" been crowded onto a Seagrave.

PHOTOS, VFD

This wood and brick hall at Duchess and Leighton protected Oak Bay until 1937 when it was closed. The building still exists as an apartment block.

No. 2 Hall Yates Street originally only had a single apparatus bay. This shot, probably taken in 1912, shows a Seagrave A.C. hose wagon serving a horse drawn steam pumper.

PHOTOS VFD

Combinations were useful rigs at single bay "outside" halls such as No. 6 Fernwood where a pumper was not available. A volunteer company at Oaklands and No. 2 Hall protected the district until this hall was built in 1911.

it into Atkinson's locker. Later, Charlie went into the Chief's office and says, "Somebody stole my goat! I don't know where it is!" When asked if they'd seen it, the boys looked all serious faced. "We're all very sorry, Charlie, about your goat." So he went at last to his locker and there was the goat going MAAAAAA. And you saw Charlie there, oh, was he mad!

The outbreak of war in August 1914 inevitably had an impact on the department with men leaving for service with the army. Replacements were hired to fill in for the duration of the conflict, the jobs of those that left being guaranteed upon their return. Not only did the war in Europe complicate things, the weather also had a hand in making things difficult.

In the first week of February 1916, Victoria suffered an extremely heavy fall of snow, which brought everything in the city to a halt. On February 2, all streetcar service was suspended and schools closed. Depths of five feet were common and drifts could be as high as ten when winds were blowing. Milk, when it could be delivered at all, was transported in sleighs, and city garbage crews were put onto snow removal to assist the beleaguered street repair workers who had been detailed to the task. The *Times* reported that the library at least was open almost as and the reading room provided a "comfortable refuge...and someday soon Victoria will enjoy full resurrection. Today she is interred beneath nearly 5 feet of snow." The newspaper computed that almost 1½ million tons of snow lay on Victoria's 5,000 acres.

The fire fighters, like everyone else, were forced to cope with the situation. Reports in the *Times* chronicled efforts to remain operational.

The Fire Department is in a serious position on account of the snow. It is doubtful if the motor apparatus could get out at all, while the number of horses for the horse apparatus has been increased to three or four horses to the engine. A hose wagon on runners has been extemporized, carrying 1500 feet of hose. A sleigh has been requisitioned for Chief Davis, it being impossible to move his automobile. What ever happens, the men will make the best effort possible, but the whole department will be happy if no call is sent in. Some of the hydrants are covered with drift snow, and the men will have to burrow to reach the hydrant and couple hose.[8]

Chief Davis remained on duty continuously from Tuesday through Thursday of that week in order to cope with the emergency. All but three of the seven outside halls and headquarters were closed down, often with snowdrifts so high the doors on the apparatus floor could not be opened. It was most important, and most feasible in the chief's opinion, to concentrate all effort on protecting the business district. The army, with troops stationed at various points in the city, offered to supply additional manpower should a fire break out. Fifty men were offered by a Lt.-Colonel Henniker for duty. Fortunately no fires occurred and as always, the city survived.

As in all cities, Victoria had some districts that presented problems in terms of fire protection. Victoria had a substantial number of mills during the World War I years, many of which supplied lumber for wartime ship construction. Shipyards such as that of the Foundation Company and Cameron-Genoa, had spread around the inner harbour. Some of the mills, partly as a consequence of war requirements for increased quantities of lumber, had become very large. The department knew it was only a

[8] *Colonist*, 2 February 1916, p. 10.

matter of time until an incident would occur. In the early hours of June 8, 1917, a fire was discovered at the Cameron Lumber Company mill just as the shift change took place at 6 o'clock. The *Colonist* reported that:

... one of the foremen saw smoke issuing from a journal on the shafting in the dynamo room. Thinking it was nothing serious, for minor blazes have often been experienced in the plant, he went outside for a small hose with which to put out the fire. When he returned, the flames had spread to an extent which showed him the necessity and advisability of turning in an alarm of fire. He had to run about thirty feet to do so and when he returned, the whole interior of the planing mill was a mass of flames which had been fed by the large amount of sawdust on the premises. Before the alarm could be responded to by the fire department, the flames had broken through the roof of the mill and [were] shooting high into the air. By the time the first motor apparatus from the fire halls reached the scene, the planing mill and box factory were doomed, and the fire had spread to the machine shop and to adjoining piles of lumber.

It was one of the hottest fires the local brigade has been called upon to cope with. Apparatus from the headquarters hall, as well as from Victoria West, Dunedin Street, and Fernwood Road halls was quickly on the spot, but lack of water hampered the efforts of the firemen. The fact that the tide was out prevented the engines from being worked from the harbor, and recourse had to be had to the hydrant on the dead end of Garbally road main, the hydrant on Selkirk Avenue some considerable distance away, and to one stream from the fire protection system installed at the mill. In all, four streams were in use where ten or twelve would not have been too many. With limited facilities, the firemen had difficulty in surrounding the fire, though it is doubtful if with treble the number, anything could have been done to save the premises.

A considerable portion of the destroyed plant was built out over water, and for hours afterwards, the fire continued in the supporting wharf and lumber piles. The sawmill at the south side of the mill premises was protected by piles of sawdust which, while they became ignited, did not burn rapidly and were kept under control by being occasionally drenched by water.[9]

Fortunately the fire was contained within an hour of the arrival of the fire department. In writing up his annual report for 1917 Chief Davis confirmed some of the problems cited in the newspaper report.

Our department had to work from an engine on a hydrant on a dead end of a six inch main. The lowness of the tide made it impossible to set our engines to take suction from the harbor, so taking all into consideration, with the three streams that were available, our department did excellent work in confining the fire in the buildings wherein it started.[10]

As if any more difficulties were needed, the department was seriously crippled by the worldwide influenza epidemic of 1918-19. Five cases of the disease occurred in the department in October 1918, with one of the firefighters dying, and a further 25 fell ill over the next two to three months, fortunately without further fatalities. The department at this time had a total strength of 66 men. The following quote from the City Health Officer's report describes the situation in Victoria generally.

This disease, which was in world-wide epidemic, made its first appearance in Victoria early in October and became most prevalent towards the end of the month, gradually subsiding until Christmas, when the number of cases began to increase. The number of cases reported being 2,759, and the number of deaths 101 ... the following measures were taken to combat the epidemic. A ban was placed on all indoor assemblies, churches, theatres, and schools were closed from

9 "Mill Fire." *Colonist*, 9 June 1917, p. 1.

10 "Report of the Chief of the Fire Department." in the *Corporation of the City of Victoria Annual Reports* 1917, p. 115.

October 8th to November 20th. Directions as to how to avoid infection and how to act if infected were published in the daily papers, and addresses given to working men. Houses where influenza occurred were placarded and the patients quarantined...[11]

Several books written by travellers to Victoria have described the city over the years. One of these, *All About Victoria*, by Alfred J. Emberson and published in 1917, describes the department as it appeared to him on a visit early in World War I. It is interesting to note that the author's background is evident in the description; some of the terminology employed in descriptions is decidedly British.

Adjoining the Public Market is the principal fire station. There are eight stations and seventy-three firemen, whose uniforms differ from the English in the helmets in being of black laquered leather, which of course have not the effective appearance of the English bright metal ones, but are said to be more serviceable and less effected by heat. Though mostly motors, there are a few three horse fire escapes. Some of the ladders are raised by spring compression, which by turning a wheel, a child could work, others by hydraulic or electrical appliances. The ladders are 65 feet and 75 feet, and with hook ladder connections suffice for the highest buildings which are fortunately limited to ten storeys or a height of about 120 feet and are fitted with outside fire escape stair cases. The white fire engines are very large and imposing.[12]

It is very interesting that the department was of such interest to a visitor and that it seemed to be taken as an indicator of sophistication.

Serious difficulties regarding the manning of the department became apparent by the fall of 1918. It became necessary to introduce a two-platoon organization, a plan recently adopted by other departments. The purpose of this system was to reduce the number of hours worked by firefighters while ensuring that adequate manpower would be available so more men had to be hired. Chief Davis, who along with his men felt that this organizational change was necessary, stood in opposition to the economy-minded council, who felt that it would be simply too expensive. It appears as though there was an attempt by some members of council to have the chief removed. The firefighters supported Davis and struck in favour of creating a two-platoon system. Ultimately, the two-platoon system was introduced but the price paid was the departure of an experienced and capable officer who had done much for the department. Disgusted, Davis resigned to join the Dominion Rubber Company in Vancouver, a firm which specialized in selling fire equipment. While this was taking place, other matters of a fundamental nature had to be seen to.

The apparatus roster was still in the process of change and, by 1919, only one seldom-used steam pumper was left in service from a maximum of five in 1911. According to a 1917 Report of the Underwriters' Association of Vancouver Island, 75 per cent of all fires in Victoria were being put out by chemical engines rather than pumpers—a good thing because the single steamer represented the entire pumping capacity of the department at that time.[13] The Victoria Fire Department had not yet introduced a motorized pumper to its roster. Vernon Stewart, who had been "Long Tom" Davis' deputy, took over as chief and very soon thereafter recommended that a gasoline pumper and a hose wagon to serve it should be acquired to replace the increasingly unreliable steam

[11] "Report of the Medical Health Officer." in the *Corporation of the City of Victoria Annual Reports 1918*, p. 89.

[12] Alfred J. Emberson. *All About Victoria.* Victoria, Victoria Press and Printing, 1917, p. 98.

[13] *Report of the Fire Department Branch of the Fire Underwriters' Association of Vancouver Island 1917 on Victoria B.C.* Victoria, Underwriters' Association, 1917, p. 20.

pumper. The purchase of such apparatus was adviseable, he pointed out, because

a piece of apparatus of this kind would effect a big economy in several particulars, especially in coal consumption (the steam fire engine will use 1,000 lbs of coal per hour when working at capacity, and it requires two tons a month for the heater to which it is connected when in quarters); then it is not necessary to have an engineer with a third class certificate to operate it; then in case of a waterfront fire it can be used instantly from the salt water without danger of a boiler foaming and consequent shutting down of an engine; and it is not necessary to wait from 10 to 15 minutes, an important factor in fighting fire, to start pumping as in the case of a steam fire engine, which requires that length of time to get up steam.[14]

Steamers, whether horse or tractor drawn, took up considerable space, and there was the added complication of having water heaters and boiler heaters. The necessary coal bunkers also took up room. Supplying the fuel to a steamer in action was a problem and it is uncertain now how coal was provided at a fire.

Even though he could easily justify the purchase of a new motor pumper, Stewart had to wait. He was therefore forced to depend on the unreliable steamer, the chemical apparatus, or in the downtown core, on the high pressure system. In the latter case, hose would simply be attached to hydrants. The purchase of Victoria's first motor pumper, a new LaFrance type 45 pumper, was finally approved in 1925 and the truck was delivered in August of that year for the then astronomical price of $12,500.[15] The purchase was justified on the basis of inadequate fire protection around the harbour and in parts of the city situated at higher elevations.

New pumpers were taken on strength to augment the solitary unit in 1929, and again in the spring of 1931—with the purchase of two large Type 245 LaFrance pumpers. At the same time a city service ladder truck by the same manufacturer, LaFrance Foamite, joined the roster. The pumpers were tested under the watchful eyes of the Insurance Underwriters and the Fire Wardens down at the harbour. Fire officials from nearby Port Angeles witnessed the test as well since their department was scheduled to receive similar apparatus. In another test, Joe Norman, a member of the Victoria Fire Department crew which, along with the LaFrance agent, took the ladder truck on a test ride out along gravelled and rutted roads to Mount Douglas, some six miles from Headquarters. The truck survived the punishment and along with the pumpers was accepted.

Few new firefighters were hired during the early 1920s (the last major infusion of manpower having taken place with the introduction of the two platoon system in 1918), but by 1925, a further ten men were taken on. Gray Russell, who had been working in Washington State on a dam project, returned home to Victoria for Christmas in December 1925. He did not want to return south and so, encountering Deputy Chief Alex Munro who lived near by, Russell asked if there were any vacancies on the department. Unfortunately, he was told, he was just too late since the ten men had been taken on recently, temporarily at least bringing the department up to strength. However, a month or two later the situation

[14] "Report of the Chief of the Fire Department." in the *Corporation of the City of Victoria Annual Reports* 1919, p. 89.

[15] "Report of the City Comptroller." in the *Corporation of the City of Victoria Annual Reports* 1925, "Schedule of General Purpose Debentures", December 31st 1925, (Fire Protection).

This streamlined Nott Universal hose wagon was purchased in 1914 and later converted to a double combination. Its front wheels had a disconcerting tendency to part company with the vehicle due to weak axle spindles.

Lieutenant Joe Lund was killed in September 1918 when too much pressure built up in a hand extinguisher and it exploded. He was attending a grass fire, a common event at that time of year.

By the late 1930s, the Seagrave aerial and its Type D tractor were considered almost dangerous and they were replaced in 1938. The holes in the solid rubber tires improved traction somewhat.   PHOTOS VFD

The band was popular with firefighters in the 1920s but interest waned when they were not permitted to travel. Gray Russell is second from the left on the top row and Chief Vernon Stewart is standing on the right.   GRAY RUSSELL

There was a less serious side to the band as well.   VFD

The Ruggles-Bickle acquired in November 1922 carried an impressive load. It served until 1949.

Two LaFrance pumpers were purchased in the 1920s. This is the second of these, a 1929 type 145. Note that it has right hand steering, a practice that continued on many pieces of fire apparatus in North America almost to the 1930s.

When circus animals per-
formed at the Pantages Theatre near No. 1 Hall, they
often spent their off duty
hours in the drill yard. The
firefighters do not seem to
mind.

Though pompier ladders, used for scaling the exterior of buildings, were carried on apparatus and
Victoria firefighters were trained in using them,
they were never employed operationally in this
city. The firefighters are shown wearing pompier
life belts.   PHOTOS VFD

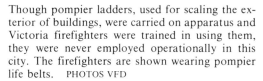

Every piece of apparatus is tested to ensure that it is up to standard. This 1931 LaFrance Type 245 pumper is shown at Victoria's Inner Harbour on March 31, 1931.

FRANK DeGRUCHY COLLECTION

Victoria Firefighter Sid Thomas.   VFD

This LaFrance is shown in 1932 shortly before receiving its windshield. Open-cabbed apparatus seldom had windshields at this time.   L. NORDLINGER, AUTHOR'S COLLECTION

Seagrave "Flatfaces" were largely relegated to reserve or were otherwise disposed of by the late 1930s. This one, however, survived long enough to take part in a Victory Bond Drive during World War II.   VFD

This 1932 photo shows details of the old Seagrave aerial. It took six men to raise the wooden ladder. Note that the tillerman's seat has been swung clear. The jumping net is mounted vertically on the far side.   VFD

A mill fire early in the morning of January 21, 1935 at the sheds of the big Canadian Puget Sound Mill.

PHOTOS, VFD

The aftermath.

Chief Alex Munroe, shown here, used this 1936 Chevy for several years.

The new Bickle-Seagrave aerial purchased in 1938 was one of the first built by that company with a metal hydraulically-raised ladder.

McALLISTER PHOTO, VFD

The 1939 fire at the Sidney Lumber warehouse on Government, in itself bad enough, would have been far worse had the gas storage tanks nearby become involved.

Irving Strickland, well-known newspaper photographer, shot this photo of firefighters H. Carter, T. Beals, and W. Holme cleaning up after a fire in the post office in the winter of 1939. Strickland recalls that frozen hydrants had to be thawed by setting fire to gasoline-soaked rags wrapped around the caps.
STRICKLAND PHOTO, VFD

The Air Raid Precautions (A.R.P.) was established in 1942. The purpose was to assist professional firefighters in the event of an enemy air attack.

Civil Defence authorities provided the A.R.P. with trailer pumps, some equipment, and turnout gear including steel helmets. On occasion, however, supplies were short and home-made gear was pressed into service.

J. Barnes and Tom Crabbe are shown instructing the A.R.P. in the use of portable pumps. There were A.R.P. first aid crews as well.   PHOTOS VFD

House fires still occurred whether it was peace or war.

Victoria and Oak Bay departments responded to this fire at the Oak Bay Sports Centre and Ice Arena on April 25, 1944, under the direction of Oak Bay Chief E. Clayards. Leaking gas filled a dressing room and the pilot light in a heater set off an explosion and fire.

This Studebaker combination protected James Bay. A converted house served as its hall 1943-1950.

PHOTOS VFD

Chief Jim Bayliss turns in an "alarm" from a callbox. These were situated at many intersections from the late 1880s until 1977. Improvements were made in the system over the years.

The box number was punched onto tape at the alarm room at headquarters and on a "repeater," as here, at an outside hall.

Alarms would also come in by phone to an outside hall. Here it is being logged. All available information was put into the record.

had changed and Gray was stopped by Munro while walking near his home. Asked if he still wanted a job with the department, the response was an enthusiastic, "I sure do!"

Unlike most new members of the department, Gray was able to avoid what had become a tradition: an initiation. Though he was fortunate in being at an outside hall at the time his was scheduled, he does, however, recall one incident that took place at Headquarters.

We used to have initiations when you were a rookie coming on. They usually set up a judge and jury. I remember one fella, Tom Crabbe, they sentenced him to be thrown out the back window of the firehall—that was on the second floor. In those days the streetcars were still running. They blindfolded him, took him into the room, and he heard them opening the window and he could hear the streetcars below. He began to struggle. There was a roof below the window and there were two guys with blankets. They pushed him, it was almost bad enough to give him heart failure. It was a great way of breaking tension—for them, not Tom.

Russell took to fire-fighting readily, although like many others, he was bothered by smoke. The only protection firefighters had at this time was a primitive breathing device in which the contaminated air passed through a carbon filter. "If you used one," he recalled, "the chief asked what was the matter with you." Though some of the men claimed that smoke did not bother them, Gray never believed that. However, if the smell and difficulty breathing were not problems, then finding your way by feel certainly was. This aspect of fire-fighting has not changed appreciably; it is still quite possible to become lost in heavy smoke or trip over objects on the floor. Stairwells and open elevator shafts increase the danger as well.

Joe Norman's experience in the 1930s was perhaps typical. He joined the department as a reliefman, serving mainly at outside halls and much of his time on the job was spent in doing routine duties around No. 8 Hall, carrying wood and coal upstairs to supply the stove, washing windows, floors, and the apparatus. Each man at the Oak Bay Hall had some privacy in that he had his own room with a single bunk but there was only a single window on the second floor looking out towards the street. Most of the time it was boring in the early 1930s, Norman recalls, but on occasion the boredom was punctuated by surprise drills when Deputy Munroe would show up unexpectedly and ring the gong. Most fires seemed to be nothing out of the ordinary but seldom were any two alike. Norman recalls some fires that he attended.

Where the Hudson's Bay Parkade is now, there used to be a number of two-storey houses. The store used to rent space in these to store mattresses. Well, they caught fire! Talk about smoke! We didn't have oxygen masks, we just choked!

In Oak Bay one rainy night, a woman's chimney caught fire. I went up to the roof and straddled the peak and pointed a hand extinguisher down the chimney. I didn't have my helmet on and a burning cinder went down my neck. I couldn't do anything or I'd slip off the roof—I had to let it burn. My partner Frank was standing on the kitchen stove trying to remove the stovepipe when the woman came in saying that the fire was coming down the living room chimney. Frank hollered to me, "Joe, take this outside!" and tossed the hot pipe to me. I juggled it and managed to get it out through the screen door to the back porch.

A frequent location of fires in the 1930s (as it still is now) was on the beach below Dallas Road. Picnickers lit bonfires and then the large quantities of driftwood later caught fire when the departing merrymakers neglected to put them out properly.

I was substituting for one of the Woodburn brothers, one of them was a fireman and the other a detective. Anyhow, he was a big son-of-a-gun, he was six foot one or two and 210 pounds, a lot bigger than me. I had to take his helmet, coat and boots. The truck went down to the beach. I took the plug and they went flying on. They gave me a blast to turn the water on and I had to stop traffic at Clover Point. Someone came along in a car and hollered "Hey, Joe! Is that you under all that?"

Joe Norman found it difficult to tolerate those periods of boredom, and there were many of them, when nothing was happening. He left the department before too long being too "full of beans" to stand around.

There were some fire hall closures in the late 1930s, the first since several resulting from motorization in 1918. This time, budgetary problems that characterized a depression economy were the cause. Oak Bay municipality, which had been protected by Victoria firefighters since the construction of the No. 8 Duchess and Leighton Hall in 1911, was finding the payments to Victoria burdensome.[16] Their response was to create their own department, enticing some Victoria firefighters to join their ranks. A twelve-year veteran of the Victoria department, Edward Clayards, became their first chief. No. 4 Hall in Vic West was closed as an economy measure, fire protection then being provided primarily from No. 5 Hall across the Point Ellice bridge augmented when necessary from Headquarters. Apparatus from No. 1 crossed the harbour via the Johnson Street bridge.

The *Colonist* of March 12, 1937 confirmed that the city viewed the fire hall closures as a means of avoiding a tax increase, a highly desirable circumstance in the hard times. Between 1931 and 1936, No. 2 Yates Street Hall had responded to 228 calls, No. 5 Burnside to 177, and during the same period, No. 4 Vic West to only 86.[17] The only justification for keeping No. 4 in operation, might have been to provide some measure of protection to Esquimalt and some of the more westerly parts of Saanich. In most instances, however, No. 5 could respond more quickly.

During the depression years it was very difficult to find a fulltime job but especially so, one with the fire department. Even with wages of firefighters having been reduced to cut costs, the prospects of steady work were all but non-existent. The reduction of the firefighters' work week from 72 to 60 hours in the mid-1930s and the later closure of halls meant that a few openings—very few—did occur. Percy Graves, who retired as a senior officer with the department, was one of the fortunate few who heard about an opening by chance, in this case from the department's mechanic who purchased parts from the garage where he was working. He applied and was accepted.

In 1937 when Percy joined the department, wages were $127 per month for a First Class Firefighter, one with three years experience. Being essentially an apprentice, he at first earned only $90, but when he passed his probationary period of six months, he noticed that he was taking home even less because of deductions. The initial training period lasted three months, during which time he worked seven days a week, often

[16] "Council to Close Hall." *Times*, 9 February 1937, p. 3.

[17] "Fire Chief Relates Reason for Closing Vic West Hall." *Colonist*, 12 March 1937, p. 2.

night shift. He was still required to be there the next morning at 8 o'clock for training. It was a trying experience but the only part of his training that really bothered him was when the aerial ladder was raised in the centre of the drill yard and it swayed back and forth in the wind.

As has been typical in every period of the department's history, practical jokes around the fire hall were very common, as Graves recalls

There were wet drills when we'd end up thoroughly soaked. Beforehand, we'd take off our underwear and socks. Afterwards one of the fellows would put his shoes out on a window sill to dry and someone would nail them down. Once they did it to the drill captain's shoes — that was a mistake! There were a number of people who would often find themselves in trouble because of their practical jokes and you'd hear "Doherty and Grace below!" Alex McAllister once planted a bucket of water above a door all set to come down when I opened it. He called me to come into the room and just as I was about to do so, a captain came by headed in the same direction. I sidestepped and he got wet! There was one fellow that we called "Wooden shoes" and we rigged his bunk to collapse. He came in, sat down took his shoes off, and then his pants. Nothing happened! We waited, then at last went over and touched the bed — the whole thing collapsed.

Life around a fire hall that shared its quarters with a public market could have its unusual aspects, said Graves.

The city used to supply us with 22 ammunition for killing rats around the market. The stalls were up about four inches above the floors so that we could turn on a hose and clean it out. There was this huge rat we saw poking its head out from under a stall. We got the gun and 'killed' it several times.

We had an elephant at the hall once — it was in an act at the Pantages [theatre]. Three or four of us used to go and stand at the back of the stage and we had a fellow who was supposed to tell us when the alarm went. Well, one night the alarm went and he didn't tell us. We came out and we heard sirens — we made it all right.

While at headquarters the firefighters were expected to get their daily exercise and the means devised was very strenuous indeed. Graves did not enjoy it much.

They used to take us out at 6:00 to the Bank of Toronto building [11 storeys high] and made us run up the fire escapes. It was hard first thing in the morning — very hard!

Bert Wilkinson, present day Deputy Chief/Operations, recalled one story that has been repeated over the years concerning Chief Munroe who took over from Vernon Stewart in 1929. Typically, during the summer months, firefighters would lean out of open second-storey windows at No. 1 and watch the girls walking down Cormorant or Broad streets just opposite the fire hall. Bored with simply watching, one of the firefighters felt that he might get more of a reaction if he could throw a potato and catch one of the girls heading south on Broad in the rear end. Just as he was winding up, potato in hand, he heard a voice behind him "And what do you think you're doing?" Recognizing the speaker, he turned slowly around to find Chief Munroe directly behind him. Quickly deciding that the truth would probably be the only acceptable answer, the firefighter described what he intended doing, all the while expecting the worst. Alex

Chief Alex Munroe.   VFD

Munroe, who had the reputation of being extremely formal, stiffened visibly—"Do you think that you can do it?" he asked. Being assured that it was possible, Munroe said "Then go ahead." Sadly, there is no record of the result.

There were a number of tools used by firefighters in the 1930s which are no longer in use today in Victoria. One such piece of equipment is the "pompier" ladder. Pompier ladders had been developed by a St. Louis Fire Engineer, Chris Hoell in the 1880s and the term "pompier" was derived from the French for firefighter. The name stuck. In cross section, the ladders are basically "L" shaped, with the short leg situated at the top and acting as a hook. The main shaft could be 8, 12 or 16 feet in length, and rungs—steps—stuck out from either side of it. Pompier ladders, which were generally built of steel reinforced wood, enabled firefighters to scale the outside of buildings to heights beyond the reach of aerial ladders. A firefighter would stand on a window ledge, grab the ladder which was passed up between his legs, and then hook the top of the window sill above. Joe Norman recalls that one problem with this was that the window above had to be broken to provide a grip for the ladder on the window frame. For this reason there was little or no training for Victoria firefighters—windows were expensive. Though apparatus continued to carry them into the 1950s, there is no record of pompier ladders having been used in the city.

In August 1938, the department tested and then accepted for service, a new Bickle Seagrave 85-foot aerial, one of the first in Canada equipped with an all-steel, hydraulically-raised ladder. The 1911 Seagrave aerial it replaced was useless and was considered dangerous long before this. Robert Bickle, the head of the Woodstock, Ontario company, came west to make certain all was as it should be with the truck. The tractor was powered by a 12-cylinder 240 hp engine.[18] The city had a first rate piece of apparatus at $22,500—an equivalent piece of equipment would likely cost 30 times the amount 50 years later.

When war broke out in 1939, it was immediately understood that airpower rather than any threat from seaward as would have been the case in the past would present the greatest threat to Victoria. This was especially evident after Pearl Harbor was attacked in December 1941. In the event of an air attack, normal standing emergency units; fire, police, etc. would not be able to cope with the large number of resulting fires and casualties. As a consequence, an organization that had been established in Britain was instituted here as well. The Air Raid Precautions or A.R.P. was formed in British Columbia to help protect civilian lives and property. Victoria's Mayor Andrew McGavin commented on this effort in his Annual Report for 1941.

[18] "New Aerial Truck Arrives." *Times*, 19 August 1938, p. 13.

[19] "Report of the Mayor." in *Corporation of the City of Victoria Annual Reports* 1941, p. 6.

At the close of the year the war spread to the Pacific, Japan attacking the United Nations without warning by her bombing of Hawaii. Our City, alike with the whole Pacific coast, is now on the front line and every precaution must be taken for our defence. Our A.R.P. organization has been strengthened and our wardens are all aware of the menace from air attack. All the city can do is being done and although we lack many items of equipment for our ARP organization, we hope that deficiencies will soon be made up and that we will be ready for any emergency.[19]

Victoria firefighters, while they officially acted in advisory capacity on occasion, were in some cases members of the A.R.P. as well. They were, though they would be called for duty with the fire department in the event of attack, still issued with the A.R.P. "kit" for fire-fighting. The City Parks Department responded to the emergency situation by allowing the A.R.P. the use of three thousand feet of garden hose in the event of an air raid. The A.R.P., with limited funds available, were still able to provide themselves with rudimentary apparatus. The possibility of water mains being broken as a result of an air attack concerned them, and so they purchased two ancient tank trucks from junk yards in order to haul water. They also had provided a number of 200-gallons per minute portable pumps and 500-gallons per minute trailer pumps. As it turned out the A.R.P. were never called upon, but had the worst happened and Victoria been attacked, they undoubtedly would have proven useful.[20] Victoria Fire Chief Alex Munroe contributed to the defence of the city by drawing up "10 Points," a manual which provided basic fire-fighting information for the A.R.P. fire suppression crews.

With a large increase in the amount and level of activity at Ogden Point and James Bay during the war; shipbuilding, and the increase in wartime housing in the district, it was necessary to improve fire protection. A house in the 400 block on Superior Street was converted to a "gerry rig" fire hall in 1943 and equipped with a single pumper, the 1934 Studebaker. That was the first fire hall in the district since the closure of the Kingston Street Hall following World War I.

The department carried on pretty much as it had during the 1930s, except that a number of firefighters left for war service, most often with the navy or air force fire services. Their jobs were protected, being guaranteed upon their return to civilian life. While they were away, their places were taken by others who were hired on a temporary basis to maintain manpower levels. There would be some changes after the war.

Chapter 5

POST WORLD WAR II DAYS

Chief Joseph Raymond, Alex Munroe's successor.   VFD

[1] "City May Obtain Used Fire Barge."
Colonist, 15 March 1945, p. 3.

Five landing craft were disposed of by the Department of National Defence as surplus in 1945 for possible use as fire barges. There is a Steamship Registration Certificate relating to the transfer of the barge *Louisa* from the Crown to the Corporation of the City of Victoria. It was subsequently given the highly imaginative name *VFD Fire Barge*.

In some respects the department in the early post-World War II period differed little from its pre-war state, having essentially the same personnel, apparatus and facilities. Firefighters who had left the department for war service returned to duty following the conflict. There was one significant change in personnel, however, and that was the retirement in 1945 of Chief Alex Munroe who had been in charge for 16 years. He was replaced by Joseph Raymond. One piece of apparatus to be used for drill purposes, a used 1937 Chevrolet, was added to the roster in 1946. This was a converted standard commercial chassis—custom-built rigs were in short supply—and the hose truck was a low-cost solution to the apparatus shortage. It was equipped with a hose bed, booster tank, pump and reel. However, one other apparatus requirement, a long standing one, was not so easily solved.

Since the early 1870s, Victoria fire chiefs had wanted the city to provide them with some means of coping with waterfront fires. It was suggested initially that a barge should be kept in readiness for fire department use— a steam pumper and crew could board it and a steam launch could tow it to the point where it was needed. Water would be pumped directly out of the harbour and hose streams turned on the burning wharf or structure from the water side. Before the James Bay bridge was built on the site of the present causeway, it was thought this same barge could be used to ferry fire apparatus to the south side of the harbour if a blaze broke out there. This would avoid the long pull around the eastern end of the harbour, an important consideration before horses were introduced to the department. The building of the bridge made this aspect of the proposal redundant, and the advantages in having firefighters who could fight a fire from the water side were, at least for a time, ignored.

It was not until 1945 that the department got its first floating apparatus in the form of a superannuated North Vancouver fire barge named the *Louisa*. A purchase price was negotiated with North Vancouver that even the economy-minded Victoria City Council could not refuse—it was offered free of charge.[1] The deal was closed and the fire barge arrived in Victoria in March 1945 under tow where it was soon demonstrated to the Fire Wardens. The firefighters, and especially the union, pressed for a full-time fire crew for the barge but the city refused, for once being correct in claiming that it was not necessary. Very few waterfront fires had occurred in the past and the city could not afford the wages for people who would not be doing much except waiting for an alarm. They might well have waited for years.

House fires inevitably account for a large percentage of alarms. Even what have become known as "heritage houses" such as "Mount Joy," are not immune from fire.

There is high pressure in fire hoses and it often takes more than one man to keep water directed on a fire.

The darkroom in the High Tone Photo
Studio above the Kresge Store caught fire
on August 21, 1946. Two LaFrance Type
245 pumpers, and the LaFrance City Service Ladder Truck, and the Bickle Seagrave aerial responded.

Fires almost always draw large crowds
and this one on Gorge road in 1948 was
no exception.

It is fire service tradition that when a firefighter dies on duty, the last piece of apparatus to which he was assigned is used to bear him to his funeral. The Studebaker is shown here in that role at the funeral of J. C. Puckey in 1945. VFD

Firefighters often work at dizzying heights. In May 1949 J. Gilles, Alf Adamson and J. Barnes brought down an injured steeplejack from a tower of Christ Church Cathedral.

W. ATKINS PHOTO, VFD

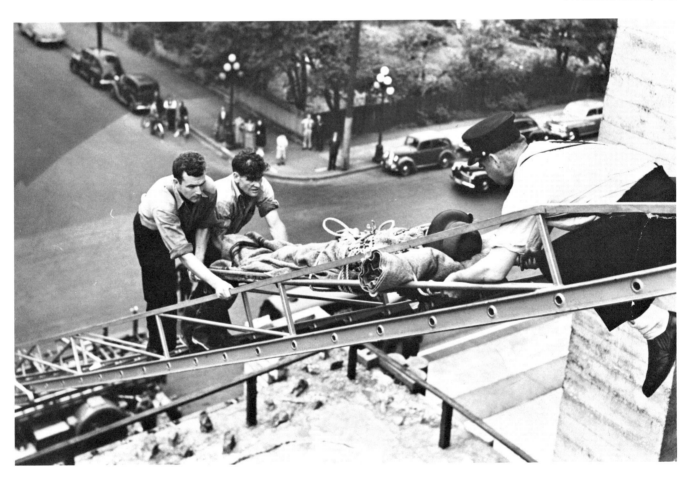

The 1937 Chevrolet hose wagon was pressed
into service for the funeral of Firefighter
Leonard Harper.

Foam has been a very effective weapon
against fires involving petroleum products
especially. First used in 1917, it deprives a
fire of oxygen.

PHOTOS VFD

One factor which made it inevitable that council would balk at providing a crew, was the reduction in the firefighters' work week from 62 to 48 hours in accordance with provincial legislation. This in itself meant that additional men would have to be taken on provide an equivalent level of fire protection generally. The thought of having to provide a full-time fire barge crew over and above this was unacceptable in council's view.[2] Instead, the council suggested they would have a volunteer crew. It was an idea which did not sit well with the firefighters, because it could be precedent-setting. The controversy raged off and on for almost a year, during which time, the barge did not have to respond to an alarm even once, and at last the decision was made to sell it. The penny-pinching attitudes of the depression years, obviously more necessary then, had continued well into the 1940s. There were, however, some hopeful signs.

In November 1948, plans were announced in the *Colonist* for the replacement of the James Bay Hall, the converted house on Superior Street that had been in operation for the previous five years.[3] Clearly, these makeshift quarters were becoming increasingly inadequate, and a new structure was to be built at the corner of Superior and Oswego streets, only about 150 feet from the existing hall. Announced also was the gradual replacement of rapidly aging apparatus. Council, at the same time, approved the purchase of a 1949 LaFrance pumper from the LaFrance Foamite company in Toronto. The new truck was intended to replace the 1925 LaFrance in front-line service, with the older rig going into reserve. At the age of 30, in 1955 the old truck was cannibalized for parts to keep the 1929 LaFrance in reserve condition. The Ruggles-Bickle ladder truck, purchased in 1922, was very old and had to be replaced. A commercial pattern G.M.C. was purchased at this time and equipped as a ladder truck, in another attempt to provide additional needed apparatus at less cost. It was found to be underpowered and was almost immediately placed in reserve. Before long "Brindle's folly" as it was unkindly named after Chief Robert Brindle, was sold to Nanaimo.

Later, on November 20, the chief was quoted in the *Times* as saying that up to five new fire halls would have to be built if Victoria was to be properly protected, some of which were, in effect, replacements for the halls closed in the late 1930s.[4] The new halls needed were: a replacement for the Cormorant Street Headquarters, inadequate since World War I; another to replace the 1908 Douglas and Dunedin Hall which had been built as No. 5 and renumbered No. 3; the converted house in James Bay, the replacement for which had been promised by Council earlier that same month; and finally, another new hall to be built in the vicinity of Stadacona Park at the eastern end of Pandora Avenue. It was to be a replacement for both the Duchess Street Hall closed in the late 1930s and the No. 2 Hall at Yates and Camosun which was by this point, 50 years old. The new hall was to protect the Royal Jubilee Hospital, situated only a block or two from the closed Duchess Hall. In his 1950 annual report, Chief F. W. Briers once again commented that

No. 2 Station, at Camosun and Yates Streets, is wrongly placed now and should be located close to the junction of Fort and Pandora where city-owned land has been reserved for the purpose. Approval for this proposed site was received from

The Capital City of British Columbia
Again Purchases
THE WORLD'S FINEST FIRE ENGINE
LAFRANCE FIRE ENGINE AND FOAMITE LIMITED

MONTREAL · TORONTO · VANCOUVER   Head Office and Factory: 115 OLD WESTON RD., TORONTO, ONT.

[2] "No Full Time Crew for Fire Barge." *Colonist*, 15 July 1945, p. 3.

[3] Council Approves Plans for New Equipment." *Colonist*, 9 November 1948, p. 3.

As seems typical of Victoria, it took time for the City to actually committ a budget. The decision to build a hall was made, yet again, in April 1950 ("James Bay to Have New Fire Hall for $15,500." *Colonist*, 18 April 1950, p. 1). Later, a bid was actually accepted ("Wardens Accept $14,800 Bid for Construction of Fire Hall." *Colonist*, 8 June 1950, p. 27).

[4] "Victoria Fire Department Will Need Three new Substations says Chief." *Times*, 20 November 1948, p. 7.

the B.C. Fire Underwriters Association in 1943. My opinion is that a double door station in a building large enough to provide for the fire alarm office with accommodation for the communications and signals workshop would be the solution.[5]

It was felt that the alarm room then situated at Headquarters and which was central to the operation of the department, should be moved into more "fire resistant" quarters.

Victoria West should also have a hall to replace No. 4, closed a decade earlier as an economy measure. There was still a requirement for a hall in this district—ideally a new structure but if not, the same building reopened. The Point Ellice or Bay Street bridge as it had become known locally, was decidedly elderly and, as a consequence, there was a 10 mph speed restriction on the span—emergency vehicles included. The memory of the Point Ellice bridge collapse of 1896 was well-known, especially to engineers and they were not about to take chances. This meant that valuable minutes of response time were lost by vehicles when answering alarms from either the Dunedin or Headquarters halls. When the bridge was to be replaced, and there was no indication that this would be soon, the bridge would have to be closed entirely during the period of construction leaving only one harbour crossing. If the Johnson Street bridge was to be inoperative at any point, and being a lift span it has occasionally been jammed in the "up" position, Vic West would be left all but isolated in terms of fire protection. Reintroducing on-site fire protection to Vic West was an intelligent suggestion but it was not to be, even when the bridge was being replaced in 1958. The other suggestions made by the chief respecting halls would be acted upon, but some would take up to 30 years. In the meantime the department had to carry on as best it could.

A Dangerous Job

There is inevitably an element of risk in training for any job that can involve danger, and fire-fighting is certainly a case in point since accidents can happen despite every precaution. On December 8, 1947, crews were carrying out ladder drill in the yard behind headquarters when a ladder carrying firefighter Leonard Harper, who had only joined the department two months earlier, suddenly began to slide downward. Unable to do anything he was tossed to the ground suffering fatal head injuries. Fortunately, fatalities among Victoria firefighters have been a rare occurrence on the job, the most recent previous occasion being on April 22, 1945 when J. C. Puckey, a veteran of the service suffered a fatal heart attack while attending a fire.

As so often happens, an event took place on May 4, 1949 which logically should have inspired greater efforts towards getting a new James Bay hall; nothing of substance had happened to this point. A resident of the Menzies Apartments, situated only a few blocks from the Superior Street Hall, stored some still-hot ashes inside her apartment in a cardboard box. The inevitable happened and a blaze was soon underway, sending the 25 residents of the 12-unit block scrambling for their lives. Fortunately for them, the fire department was on the scene quickly and was able to prevent the fire from engulfing the entire structure. Fire

[5] British Columbia Underwriters' Association Report on the City of Victoria, B.C. September 1951, p. 1.

The new James Bay Hall opened for public inspection in 1950. Various pieces of apparatus have served there since this 1931 LaFrance. The hall became No. 2 Hall in the 1970s. It has survived several attempts by economy-minded politicians to have it closed.

Part of the roster at No. 1 Hall in the late 1940s. The new LaFrance pumper received in 1949 is second from the left. Compare this shot with those of the same building almost half-a-century earlier (see page 66).

PHOTOS VFD

Chief Robert Brindle.   VFD

The Ruggles service truck was totally obsolescent by the mid-1940s. Chief Brindle's answer to the problem was a 1949 G.M.C. with a locally built body. It was found to be underpowered and was sold to Nanaimo, and, perhaps unkindly, became known as "Brindle's Folly."

FRANK DeGRUCHY

This photo, one of Frank DeGruchy's favourites, shows the truck on the right with Ansul chemical tank. Before long its pump was removed. The firefighters are presently searching out parts for its restoration.

FRANK DEGRUCHY

"The Battle Joined!"

The deep sea tug *Salvage King* caught fire while along-side the wharf in Victoria Harbour. Shipboard fires are difficult and dangerous to fight. Ironically, the ship had recently been equipped for firefighting.

STRICKLAND PHOTO, VFD

Capitulation!

The harbour tug *Island Trooper* was equipped with powerful pumps and monitors.

VFD

Some fires involving vessels can be fought with relative ease from wharves. This one in 1962 was situated at the old Fisherman's Wharf below the Johnson Street Bridge.

PHOTOS VFD

These small wooden "double-enders" were fire traps. Once retired, they often served as floating homes.

Warden Alderman John Baxter was quick to point out in the press that on the basis of this fire, the decision of the Wardens to continue the presence of the department in the district had been a good one.[6] The hall ultimately was built and opened on November 22, 1950, but it would have to weather repeated attempts to close it down in the future.

Rescues, often carried out at great heights, are an integral and almost routine aspect of fire-fighting. In May 1949, a steeplejack named Harrison was at work on the south tower of Christ Church Cathedral when he slipped, sustaining severe injuries. The 1938 Seagrave aerial was sent to the scene and its 85-foot steel ladder was extended to the top of the tower. Firefighters J. Gilles, Alf Adamson, and J. Barnes were able to secure the injured man to a "Dunn" stretcher which was designed to be used with the aerial ladder. The injured man was slid down the ladder without further incident. Twenty-seven years later, Adamson was surprised that anyone would consider the incident as being anything other than routine.

The insurance industry has long had an interest in fire protection in Victoria as we have seen from earlier chapters. The Fire Department branch of the British Columbia Underwriters' Association took a very active role in ensuring that high standards were maintained, assessing the performance of personnel and apparatus, and the state of all facilities affecting fire protection. These investigations are carried out with the full co-operation of the city and the department, and result in detailed reports issued at set intervals, generally two years. In September 1951, the Association issued a report which included, as was standard practice, a detailed description of the city as well as those concerns specifically relating to fire protection.

Victoria, in 1951, according to the report, had a population of 61,420, a figure which excluded the other "core"—those making up Greater Victoria—municipalities of Esquimalt, Saanich, and Oak Bay. The city occupied a land area of 7.5 square miles, with all but 10 per cent of this being developed.[7] The remainder of the land was as yet undeveloped or devoted to recreational use. A number of other factors had to be considered if a complete picture was to be provided.

Unlike the situation today, most homes in Victoria during the early 1950s were heated by wood, sawdust, fuel oil or manufactured gas, each one of which, if used carelessly, was potentially dangerous. Other problems were facing the fire department as well, such as the presence of paint and varnish and roofing material factories, both industries which dealt with highly flammable materials. Fortunately there were no plants situated in a residential area. Sidney Roofing was provided with its own alarm box connected to the Fire Department as a precaution from 1950. It did not help much and the company's facilities were in fact destroyed by fire on March 27, 1960.

The "weapons" available to the department were also described in detail in the report—exhaustively so to all but the most dedicated reader. Water was one aspect of the situation that was thoroughly investigated. Briefly, the Greater Victoria Water District was created by provincial legislation in January 1949. The water supply for all uses and, particularly for this study, fire-fighting, were from this point controlled by an inter-municipal board which apportioned the water resources between each of

[6] "New Fire Hall in James Bay a Wise Act." *Colonist*, 6 May 1949, p. 6.

[7] "Underwriters' Report 1951," p. .

its members.[8] It was certainly a more efficient way of operating with much less chance of a general shortage. Yet some aspects of the situation still were causing some concern.

A very thorough investigation indicated that while water supplies were reliable and "adequate," the quantities available in some locations might be insufficient in the event of a major blaze. The department in such circumstances would quickly if temporarily overtax the water supply. It was obvious that fires would not break out only in areas that were well protected. The "High Value District," the business district downtown, was protected by the high pressure system installed before World War I. The state of the alarm system caused some concern as well when it was discovered that some of the wiring was in poor condition and subject to exposure from power lines, possibly leading to short circuits and false alarms, and two circuits were grossly overloaded. Some of the box alarms were of a decidedly inferior, very old type and were potentially unreliable. Tests and inspections of the system, not only at the Hadquarters and outside halls, but throughout the entire system, were too infrequent due to insufficient manpower.[9]

Victoria simply had too few firefighters. Apparatus responded to alarms with insufficient men, a situation which could lead to serious safety problems as well as less efficiency when fighting the fire. The report came out strongly in favour of hiring additional ladder, pumper and hose companies, which would, if introduced, bring the department up to an efficient and safe level. The apparatus, while kept in good condition by the department's mechanical department, was obsolescent and therefore badly in need of replacement—the 1949 LaFrance pumper was the only up-to-date piece of apparatus on strength. Moreover, a fireboat service in some form was still needed. There had not been any thought given to a replacement for the barge and waterborne fire protection was rated by the Underwriters as being "deficient." In 1950, though informal, steps had been taken to mitigate the problem. Chief Briers wrote in his report that

We have a "verbal understanding" with the Pacific Salvage Company, owners of the *Salvage King*, which is equipped with fire pumps of 3,000 gallons capacity, with deck monitors, to assist in fighting a major fire on the waterfront, on our request. Members of the Department would be placed on this boat to direct the fire streams. The officers and men have visited the boat to familiarize themselves with the equipment. The big disadvantage is that the *Salvage King* is frequently absent for extended periods.[10]

The report continued, stating that the response to alarms was "not well arranged," however, training and discipline and the fire suppression methods employed, were rated "very good" as was the performance of the inspection branch. Victoria's fire halls were generally well-rated with the exception of the half-century-old headquarters hall. The building itself was a fire hazard.

Chief F. W. Briers, who likely knew the contents of the report before it was actually issued, was attempting to implement some of its recommendations in the spring of 1951. No doubt on the basis of his own experience rather than any specific recommendation in the report, he wanted an additional 20 men. Unfortunately, his efforts coincided with the awarding

[8] "Underwriters' Report 1951," p. 3.

[9] "Underwriters' Report 1951," p. 27.

[10] "Waterfront Protection." *Report of the Chief of the Fire Department 1951*, p. 6.

The Annual Reports of the Fire Department as included in the *Corporation of the City of Victoria Annual Reports* were all but useless in terms of the information presented. This is true from the mid-1940s to date, and so the Department's official reports of its activities were used from c. 1950 for information.

A good portion of Victoria's industry was located on the waterfront
and so many serious fires could be fought from both the land and
water sides. *Above*: Modestly hiding behind a piling, the *Island
Trooper* directs its monitors towards the Selkirk Mill site. That is
B.C. Forest Products can be seen in the background.

Captain Harold Elworthy of Island Tug and Barge shows *Island
Comet*'s deck monitor to Chief Frank Briers.

PHOTOS VFD

The *Island Comet* was soon unofficially dubbed the "Island Crumpet."

Fireboats were called into action at the McCarter Shingle Mill warehouse fire in 1954. It was fought from both sides.

The "Crumpet," despite being a small vessel, could produce an enormous amount of water. The supply was unlimited.

The fire at the Mount Douglas Apartments at the Oak Bay Junction proved difficult because of the number of elderly people involved.

There were differences between the Victoria and Seattle trucks, most of which represented department preferences. The position of the booster reel was different on the Seattle truck and there were compartments situated below the hard suction hoses.

This Seattle Fire Department Kenworth pumper served as a prototype for Victoria's rigs.

The Kenworth ladder truck was an impressive piece of apparatus employing a locally designed and built body on a chassis purchased in Seattle. The truck had a 500 gallon booster tank and reel in addition to its full complement of ladders and hooks. It was the modern equivalent of the Union Hook and Ladder apparatus used over a hundred years earlier.

PHOTOS VFD

by arbitration of a 12 per cent wage increase in April 1951, a move intended to bring Victoria firefighters more in line with others elsewhere in the province.[11] Predictably, the city council's reaction to the award was to threaten staff reductions.

The *Colonist* of April 8, 1951, reported the events at a meeting of the Fire Wardens held the previous day, in which Alderman Aubrey Kent remarked that "the only solution seems to be a cut in staff. The City can't stand all these extra costs (the wage increase)."[12] His view clearly ran counter to that of the Underwriters which would appear some months later. Alderman Baxter, who in 1949 had supported the department's attempt to get a new James Bay hall, spoke out against any increase in manpower. The level of fire protection to be provided seemed all but irrelevant in the face of financial considerations.

The dispute was to smoulder without actual cuts taking place over the next year, finally reaching its climax in April/May 1952. Before this, however, Chief Briers had to face a problem that has plagued firefighters since the earliest days of the department — "miniature incendiaries." The *Colonist* on April 5, 1952, reported that two little "firebugs" had set fire to a shed. Having succeeded in getting a good blaze going, they then threw on some tires which gave off a very satisfying black smoke. The fire was soon out of hand and the arsonists fled. It was not long before the fire department arrived after successfully negotiating the heavy noon-hour traffic. The fire was soon out and an investigation was underway. Within a few minutes, Chief Briers was approached by a small boy. The newspaper report continued.

Another four year old proceeded to squeal on his two pals. "Show me!" said the gasping fire chief. Hand in hand, the fire chief walked across the street to a neighbour's house. They searched all over until they came to a small divan. "Under there!" exclaimed the youngster proudly. With a gleam in his eye, Chief Briers got down on his hands and knees to look. The space was empty. He turned to his informer who was backing up. "Well?" "They must be outside," the tiny voice said. They were! If the chief's recommendations to their parents are carried out, the children will be eating their breakfasts standing up.

On April 8, 1952, there were hints of more trouble on the way from the seemingly ever-penurious council. The press reported comments that a second recently awarded pay increase of 17 per cent might well result in an increase in the mill rate.[13] Some members of council were utterly outraged at the arbitration award, seeming to take it almost as a personal affront. As in the late 1930s, fire halls and jobs were to be sacrificed irrespective of the fact that the Underwriters' report had recommended otherwise.

On April 30, 1952, council had before it a motion to close No. 2 Hall on Yates Street, a move that would mean the loss of badly needed fire protection in the district, and the loss of 14 jobs. Already undermanned, the department would find the task of protecting Victoria even more difficult. Alderman Waldo Skillings calculated that the city would save $30,000, for the remainder of 1952, and taxpayers could look forward to a $55,000 reduction in future budgets with the closure.[14] Chief Briers reacted angrily, especially when it was suggested that the recently ordered Kenworth pumper chassis then being completed with a Victoria-built

[11] "Fire Department Facing Staff Cuts." *Colonist*, 8 April 1951, p. 1.

[12] *Colonist*, 8 April 1951, p. 1.

[13] "Mill Rate Increase Possible for City." *Colonist*, 8 April 1952, p. 1.

[14] "City Will Close One Fire Hall: 14 out of Work." *Colonist*, 30 April 1952, p. 1.

body in the City Public Works yard would more than fill the gap left by the laid off firefighters and No. 2 Hall. Proof of the statement seemed to be that $21,500 was paid for the new truck—everything seemed to be "dollars and cents." Skillings, almost livid over the wage increases, went so far as to suggest further reductions and said there was no need to have highly paid, unionized firefighters manning the alarm and telephone systems. In his opinion a civilian who would be paid less could do it equally well.

Things briefly took an even more discouraging turn in the first week of May 1952—there were proposals from other members of council that not only should No. 2 be closed, but No. 3 should also cease operation.[15] In their view, it would be less expensive to hire the Saanich Fire Department under contract to protect the combined industrial and residential district. This was a foolish suggestion, since such a proposal, if put into force, would add vital minutes to response time irrespective of whether or not there were financial benefits. It received the attention it deserved. Skillings was, in any case, putting all his energy into closing No. 2.

Chief Briers was quoted in the newspapers as having sent council a letter in which he stated that "they [the council] will be responsible for loss of life or anything else from then on. They're not holding me responsible!"[16] The next day, May 7, council voted 7-4 in favour of the closure, the Mayor voting against the motion. It was decided that No. 2 would cease to be an operational component of the fire department as of midnight May 31, 1952, and the 14 firefighters would, as feared, be laid off.

Forty members of Local 730 International Association of Firefighters had attended the lengthy council meeting but their presence did not succeed in changing the situation. Alderman Murdock, in a desperate attempt to save the hall and the firefighters' jobs, suggested that instead of closing the hall, $40,000 simply be cut from the department's budget, or alternatively, that the purchase of a new pumper be cancelled.[17] The first suggestion would probably have had the result it was intended to avoid, and the second was dismissed. Skillings felt that possibly only ten firefighters rather than 14 might lose their jobs because a crew—four men—would be needed to man the new pumper. That at least was cause for some optimism.

The firefighters received considerable support from the public, not surprisingly mostly from people in the district most directly affected. Numerous letters to the editor appeared in the press. The one below appeared in the *Colonist* on May 6, 1952, and was fairly typical.

Sir:

It would seem unwise to cut the staff of the fire department over and above the qualified expertise of the head of the department's say so. It was only a short time ago he asked and still asks for more men.

Would the council members stop paying car, fire, and life insurance to save themselves a few hundred dollars? Certainly not!

Was not the instigator of this foolish move of closing the firehall not attending a civil defence course in Ottawa a few weeks ago? If so, what is the prime factor of civil defence? Firefighting, of course.

[15] "Plan Mooted to Wipe Out Second Hall in City." *Colonist*, 1 May 1952, p. 1.

[16] *Colonist*, 1 May 1952, p. 1.

[17] "Elimination of Fire Hall Confirmed in 7-4 Vote of Council." *Colonist*, 2 May, 1952, p. 1.

Also in recent weeks it has been noted that the usual harmony and goodwill that prevailed in city hall is overshadowed by the ever prevalent axe swinging methods of the present council.

> Archie Gilles
> Jack Parrot
> Victoria

The insurance companies reacted to the situation by suggesting in the newspapers that insurance rates in the area must inevitably increase with the closure of the hall. The Victoria Trades Labour Council reacted as well, throwing its support squarely behind the firefighters. Many civic workers were concerned that wage cuts and layoffs, if they could be applied to an essential service, might well be their lot as well.

Skillings had suggested, on May 7, that his motion to close the hall might be withdrawn if firefighters were to co-operate and back down from their legally awarded wage increase. Clearly financial considerations, and possibly personal biases were at work. All the time this was going on Skillings claimed that "We don't think for one minute that there is a surplus of firemen now." All efforts to save the hall resulted in failure and the threatened closure took place on schedule. Ten badly needed firefighters were laid off.

There were subsequent attempts to reopen or replace the hall over the remainder of 1952, but the department was lacking a presence in the district until April 1959 when a new headquarters hall was opened across the road from No. 2. The closure left a legacy of bad feeling that has persisted to the present day, and wage negotiations have as a consequence been far less amicable than might otherwise have been the case. The city did not learn, and there have been further attempts at retrenchment, both in terms of manpower and the number of halls over the years.

Fortunately, there were additional purchases of apparatus during this period. The first Kenworth pumper, which, except for the chassis, had been built and equipped in Victoria to a Seattle design, was completed and assigned to the James Bay Hall in June 1952, having passed all of its tests. This rig was joined by a second Kenworth pumper in 1953, and in 1954, a third Kenworth, a service/ladder truck, joined the department. The last vehicle also had a Victoria-designed and built body on a Seattle-built chassis. While recognizing that the apparatus was needed, the ever vigilant council economized and had the bodies of the trucks built and equipped in the City Public Works yard. This made sense because under the current drive for economy it was less expensive to have them built locally, and the city received excellent apparatus which would serve into the 1970s.

As noted, one recommendation of the Underwriters' 1951 report was the provision of a fireboat for Victoria, notwithstanding the barge debacle of the mid-1940s.[18] It fell to a local towboat firm, Island Tug and Barge, to equip a number of its tugs with fire-fighting pumps, hoses and monitors at its own expense as well as Pacific Salvage which, as mentioned, equipped the large deep-sea tug *Salvage King*. The vessel was touted by its owners as a veritable fire-fighting arsenal in its own right, and though this was quite accurate, it was a fact which did little to render the ship suitable for fighting one of the city's most serious waterfront fires.

18 "Underwriters' Report 1951," p. 42.

At about 7:30 a.m. on October 19, 1953, a fire broke out in the vicinity of the messboy's cabin on board the *Salvage King* which was tied up near what would become the Black Ball Ferry wharf. The fire spread quickly below decks, and three crewmen on board were powerless to prevent its spread. A *Times* article describing the blaze reported that

Firemen and Island Tug and Barge crews fought vainly ... to reach the stubborn fire which burned fiercely in bedding, stores, rubber hose, rope and salvage gear. Hundreds of thousands of gallons of water were poured into the hull in an attempt to let firemen reach the seat of the blaze ...[19]

An attempt was made to cut through the wooden hull of the ship but this was abandoned when the steel inner hull was encountered. Efforts were then turned towards cutting two holes in the foc's'le with torches from the ship's salvage gear, through which water could be pumped. While all this was going on, a monitor was removed from *Island Trooper*, a small harbour tug, and directed at the hot decks of *Salvage King*, from atop the stricken tug's bridge. At 11:40, Chief Briers ordered his crews off the tug, it being obvious that efforts to save the ship were unsuccessful. Forty minutes later, the tug settled to the bottom of the harbour as a huge hissing cloud of steam rose skyward. It was all over. The tug was raised but was so badly damaged that within two years of the fire it was partially scrapped and then abandoned at Royston as part of a breakwater.

Ship fires are extremely dangerous for firefighters, particularly for those not familiar with the layout of ships. Visibility is often very poor or non-existent, and it is possible to trip over deck fittings, or to become lost below decks. It is also very easy to become trapped. Burning paint gives off toxic fumes and extremely dense smoke, which can be very unnerving in cramped unfamiliar spaces. While fireboats are certainly of use in instances like that involving *Salvage King*, they are most often used in fighting fires on shore from the water, giving a "two-pronged" attack. Such an incident was soon to occur.

Captain V. A. Schade, skipper of *Island Trooper*, the same tug that had fought the *Salvage King* fire, was guiding a barge up to the Victoria Machinery Depot Wharf at Ogden Point. It was January 13, 1954, and the day shift at the shipyard had left only a half hour earlier at 4:30 p.m. Later, Captain Schade described events from his perspective.

We spotted a glow at V.M.D. and there was a big belch of smoke and then a big belch of flame. It went a couple of hundred feet into the air. I radioed our office and asked them to call V.M.D. at once to check it, and then I let go the barge and started using my monitor.[20]

The fire seemed to be centred in the first-aid room, which, serious in itself, was further complicated by the fact that the room was situated in Pier Building No. 2, a building used to house highly flammable ship-builders' stores. The fire department was at the scene quickly, laying hose from every available hydrant on site. Just as firefighters entered the structure, five-gallon cans of paint began to explode — the firemen ran for it. When these bursts subsided, they re-entered the building only to be driven out once again as oil-fuel drums began to explode. As viewed from the Vic West side of the harbour, there would be a flash, and then

[19] "*Salvage King* Burns, Sinks. 5 Hour Fight Futile." *Times*, 19 October 1953, p. 1.

[20] "Blast-Fed Fire Rips VMD Pier." *Times*, 13 January 1954, p. 1.

Firefighters and mill workers tackled a major fire at the Hudson Lumber Company on Garbally Road in 1951. Eyewitnesses reported a muffled explosion and the rapid spread of fire which totally destroyed the sawmill within an hour.

PHOTOS VFD

While B.C. Electric line crews took care of the power lines, B.C. Forest Products watered down their stockyard to prevent the blaze spreading.

Eighty-five firefighters and five pieces of fire apparatus were needed at the Central Cartage warehouse on July 18, 1954. The roof had just collapsed into the fourth floor causing heavy damage to furniture and appliances stored in the building.

STRICKLAND PHOTO, VFD

B.C. Forest Products is in the right foreground.   VFD

Early in the morning of April 3, 1954, a fire broke out in the warehouse of the McCarter Shingle Mill. The fire was reported at roughly 2:30 a.m. Efforts were being made to prevent the fire spreading to the adjacent Lemon Gonnason yard.   VFD

Heavy smoke, sheer misery for many firefighters, was characteristic of mill fires. Here at the McCarter storage sheds, the smoke given off by burning cedar shingles was poisonous.   VFD

Fires can be fascinating for children, and this group showed up early that same morning to watch the events at the mill.
VFD

"Can you hear me?" Radio communication greatly improved the despatching of fire apparatus, even though only chiefs' cars were initially equipped.
PHOTO BY KEN, VFD

The Seagrave aerial and the 1962 LaFrance at the MacDonald's Furniture fire at Pandora and Broad Streets in 1964.

FRANK DE GRUCHY PHOTOS

The Kenworth pumper hard at work at the same fire. The hood is raised and the radiator louvres are open for engine cooling.

The 1949 LaFrance at a night fire.

The Anderson-Mack on arrival
in Victoria in the fall of 1986.
At this point, it is yet to be
lettered. Currently, it is serving
as the No. 1 Pump.

The NATECS system of intersection control introduced in the late 1950s, intended to clear traffic from intersections before the arrival of apparatus, would not work and was soon removed. It was replaced by RADOLITE.

The Yates and Cook intersection was one of the first equipped with the NATECS system and, later, RADOLITE. The latter proved successful and was used for a number of years.

PHOTOS WILLIAM A. BOUCHER VFD

A link with the past was destroyed when the last of the "Bird Cages" burned down on March 27, 1957.

PHOTOS, VFD

Don Thompson arrived for shift in time to water down the remains of the old colonial legislative building. Fortunately, sparks from the burning Assembly Hall did not start secondary fires in the vicinity.

Vice-regal mansions, the homes of the Lieutenant Governors, were not immune from fire. Built in 1860, and sold to the colonial government five years later, Carey Castle was destroyed by fire in May 1899.   PABC A2658

Only the Ballroom and Conservatory were saved.   PABC G2606

The Samuel Maclure/Francis Rattenbury-designed replacement for Government House was completed in 1903 and suffered the same fate in April 1957.
PABC B9623

The 54-year-old structure burned furiously with flames being seen clearly in Port Angeles, WA, 18 miles away across the Strait of Juan de Fuca. There was considerable fear that the fire would spread to tinder dry trees in the district as sparks shot into the air when the roof and walls collapsed.   PABC

"Came dawn April 15, 1957." Just ashes and charred debris remain.   VFD

By the late 1950s, the necessity of a new No. 1 Hall became apparent even to the politicians. The old Market Building hall was itself a fire trap. The new hall shown here was located closer to the geographic centre of the city even though it was some distance from the business core.

PHOTOS, VFD

On February 27, 1960, one of the more spectacular of Victoria's many mill fires broke out at the Crowe Gonnason (formerly Lemon Gonnason) mill. The tinder-dry, 50-year-old buildings burned furiously sending dense smoke into the air and attracting large crowds of spectators. The Kenworth service truck is shown at the main entrance to the mill on Government, not far from where the Sidney Lumber Yard burned in the 1930s.

Moving hose is heavy work.   VFD

The Crowe Gonnason fire from another angle.   STRICKLAND PHOTO, VFD

Totally involved.   IAN McKAIN PHOTO VFD

Water turns immediately to steam as it hits the blazing structure.

Left hand page:
Streams are played on the blazing structure with a Kenworth pumper in the foreground. The age of the buildings is apparent in this photo.

STRICKLAND PHOTO, VFD

Chief Jim Bayliss in command at the Crowe Gonnason fire.

WILLIAM A. BOUCHER PHOTO, VFD

Right:
The metal roof is curling from the heat as the structure appears ready to collapse.

STRICKLAND PHOTO, VFD

Reversed helmets protected eyes from heat. Gray Russell is in the background. It often takes two men to keep the stream of water directed to where it is intended.

WILLIAM A. BOUCHER PHOTO, VFD

Several lines serve or supply a monitor. Until recently, these were generally difficult to use being carried high on the truck, often between booster reels and just forward of the hose bed where they were difficult to remove.

something would be hurled into the air before the report of the explosion reached the viewpoint approximately half-a-mile to the north. The author, at this time eight years old, witnessed the fire from this point.

What really concerned the firefighters, however, was not the paint or the oil, but rather two transformers which supplied power for machinery on the pier and to ships that berthed alongside. The transformers contained tar and oil, both of which would burn fiercely once started and be very difficult to extinguish. Hoses were kept trained on the transformers with blue and white flashes being given off as water hit exposed wires. There was the fear too that acetylene tanks stored in the building might explode but fortunately this at least did not happen. The passenger ferry *Island Princess* which was tied up nearby, was threatened until the *Island Planet*, another Island Tug and Barge tug, arrived and towed the vessel clear. Had that ship caught fire, there was a chance that the fire would have spread much further. The navy had a new destroyer escort under construction only a short distance away.

Island Planet had brought over the company's fire barge, the *Sadie II*. Normally used to wash out the company's barges, its monitors were soon turned on the fire. Later, when it was used to knock down a wall before it could fall on anyone, the stream of water knocked three firefighters to the ground very nearly washing them off the wharf into the ice-cold water of the harbour. The navy responded with a pumper, which was used to produce foam, and its No. 2 Fireboat from the base at Esquimalt. A navy fire service officer directed the fireboat by radio from a car on shore. At about 6:25, there was a rumble and firefighters at work on the east side of the pier ran for safety as a wall fell just inches from where they had been standing.

Mayor Claude Harrison was very impressed by the performance of the fireboats and was reported as commenting that "I think we should have a fireboat. It's just good luck we got out of that fire. We've been lucky with two—you can't tell about a third. Elworthy's boat is an excellent thing. It shows the value of a fireboat. I still favour having one of our own." This was not to be, however, but the city formalized their arrangement with Island Tug and Barge on September 23, 1955.[21] By 1962, three fire tugs were being operated by the Company: *Island Trooper* (750 gallons per minute), *Island Comet* (1,800 gallons per minute), and *Island Rocket* (1,800 gallons per minute). These were simply harbour tugs equipped with fire-fighting pumps and monitors which would only be used as such in an emergency. Waterborne firefighters would be called into action again, a particularly noteworthy instance being a major fire at Ogden Point in August 1977.

In Chief Briers' view it was the "worst and most dangerous" fire the department had ever had. Had there been a wind, the blaze might well have spread all the way downtown. As it turned out, it was a spectacular though not especially costly blaze, the final figure being roughly $60,000 in damages. There were soon to be far costlier blazes and in more than a strictly financial sense.

One of the last vestiges of British Columbia's Colonial past, a portion of what had been known as the "Bird Cages," had survived almost a century and was by the late-1950s being used as a meeting hall. Originally

[21] "Waterfront Protection," *Report of the Chief of the Fire Department*, 1955.

used to house the colonial and early provincial Legislative Assembly, the wooden-frame structure was situated behind its 1897-vintage replacement, the present legislative buildings.

A civil defence meeting had broken up shortly after 11:00 p.m. on March 27, 1957, and the building cleared. Slightly more than an hour later, the caretaker in the legislative building, purely by chance, looked out towards the south and to his horror the building seemed to explode in a solid pillar of flame. From other points in the city people thought the legislative building, only a few feet from the old assembly hall, had gone up. The fire had achieved quite a hold on the structure before it made its presence known. Within 45 minutes of its discovery, the ceiling beams and sections of roof came crashing down sending sparks and glass all over the neighbourhood. It was necessary to position fire lookouts nearby to guard against secondary fires starting in any of the wood buildings or residences typical of the district. Firemen turned their hoses on the south section of the building and took some lines inside, soon being forced out again by the searing heat. The protective clothing of one firefighter caught fire and his colleagues had to roll him on the ground to smother the flames. The heritage structure was soon completely destroyed.

One amusing sidelight to an otherwise serious incident was provided by a drunk who repeatedly, and with considerable determination, attempted to "assist" firefighters. The fire department did not find the situation amusing and the police ultimately had to remove him. Once both daylight and sobriety returned, the "apprentice smoke eater" was fined ten dollars.

Government House, the official residence of the province's Lieutenant-Governor and a heritage structure in its own right, was to provide the department with another major exercise in futility only three weeks later. A "first alarm" was turned in by a night watchman at 4:14 a.m. on April 15, 1957, a short time after attempts by the staff to bring the blaze under control themselves. As is often the case at this time of year in Victoria, a heavy wind was blowing and this added to the problems faced by the firefighters. Reporter Erith Smith described what happened.

Helped by the airy spaciousness of the ballroom, halls and reception rooms, the wind pushed the flames from room to room and from wall to wall. Tons of water cascaded into the flames to vanish as if they'd never been.... Every few minutes there was a warning shout and a crash audible above the roar of fire pumps as sections of roof and wall thundered down. More and more as the hours went by, the firemen concentrated on the east wing, which had contained kitchen, butler's pantry, and some servants' quarters.[22]

The west wing, with its Royal apartments, and the central portion of the building were soon gone. Present Deputy Chief Bert Wilkinson was one of the 89 firefighters battling the blaze and he recalls that Chief Briers ordered hoses turned on glowing embers in the centre portion of the building. There was no apparent effect from all the water, a fact that puzzled the chief. He soon realized that there was a good reason for his lack of success — he had been attempting to extinguish the lights of Port Angeles, Washington, 18 miles away across the Strait of Juan de Fuca to

[22] "Government House to be Rebuilt," *Colonist*, 16 April, 1957, p. 10.

the south of Victoria. The back of the building had been burnt away giving a clear view of the American town.

Showers of sparks were being carried into the air by the winds, and towards other houses in the district and a stand of trees adjacent to the disintegrating mansion. If the trees caught fire, then there would be a catastrophe. Preparations were made to evacuate nearby homes. Fortunately there was no need. A neighbour, Mrs. McKenzie, complimented the department for its efforts, as did Mayor Percy Scurrah: "There is an example of a fire that no one could have stopped," he said, "a 53-year-old building, tinder dry, on top of a hill with a wind from the sea. . . . I don't care how many men, how much equipment could have been mustered, they couldn't have stopped it."[23] The Rattenbury-designed structure, which had been completed in 1903, was a total loss, the cost coming to approximately a million dollars including contents. With a second historic structure destroyed in only a month, there were suggestions that arsonists might be at work and the safety of other "Heritage Firetraps" such as Helmcken House should be investigated. Fortunately the concerns proved unfounded since both fires were subsequently proven to be accidental. The government announced plans within days to rebuild the vice-regal mansion but until this was accomplished, the Lieutenant-Governor simply made arrangements to carry on, using the Empress Hotel for official functions. Although the motivation was quite different, the fire department was soon to be in new quarters as well.

By the late 1950s, the city was at last willing to recognize that the old Headquarters Hall on Cormorant Street was totally inadequate for virtually any use. Approval was given to acquire land opposite the closed No. 2 Hall, and following some controversy as to which property would be chosen, construction began. The new location of Headquarters would provide far better protection to both the downtown core, since there would be less of a problem with traffic congestion, and to the Royal Jubilee Hospital/Veteran's Hospital complex. With the closure of both the Duchess Hall in the late 1930s and that of No. 2 in 1952, all calls from this area had been handled from Headquarters, a fact which dramatically increased response time simply because of the increased distance involved. With the new Headquarters Hall being situated on a main arterial, responding to calls in the central business district was simplified even though distances, and heavy traffic had increased.

Clearing a Path

The department had always been concerned about public safety when responding to alarms and various attempts were made to ensure that accidents would not occur in intersections. Ideally they should be cleared of traffic before fire apparatus reached them. One partial solution that worked for a time around 1917, was to have warning horns, which were electrically operated, placed at major intersections. They were activated for a period of two minutes as the apparatus left the Cormorant Street Hall. In this period before the introduction of traffic signals there had to be some way of warning the public. As traffic volume increased, the sound of the horns was often drowned out with the result that the devices

[23] *Colonist*, 16 April 1957, p. 10.

Chief J. Bayliss and a Rad-O-Lite transmitter. VFD

were removed after a few years. By the mid-1950s, there were attempts to control traffic signals by radio devices, because a landline from the fire hall to traffic signals was considered too expensive. The move of the Headquarters Hall to its present location on upper Yates Street made several changes in emergency routes necessary.

In 1958, the microwave-activated NATECS system was introduced on a trial basis with transmitters experimentally fitted to some apparatus and receivers to traffic signals. The system did not work, with even the manufacturer at last giving up and removing it, thus leaving the department without any means of clearing intersections.[24] There was talk of going back to a wire control system; however, this was impractical because of the cost. In 1962, a new system called Rad-O-Lite was installed and satisfactorily tested, first being used on the important Vic West-Industrial route. All vehicles were equipped by January 1962.

From the early 1980s, the department has equipped its apparatus with strobe lights generally mounted on the front of the vehicle or in the centre of the light bar. The flashing of these high intensity lights, even in unfavourable lighting conditions is intense enough to activate Opticom light sensors mounted on lamp standards. These change traffic signals to green immediately ahead of the apparatus clearing the intersections of traffic in the direction of travel. The drivers, because the strobe lights make the trucks more visible, generally turn them on even when not proceeding along an Opticom-equipped route. The system is superior to the radio activated Radolite signal changer in that once the apparatus has passed, the signals will return automatically to normal operation.

New Apparatus

New apparatus was acquired in the 1960s. A 1962 LaFrance pumper replaced its remaining 1931 equivalent, and in December 1964, it was announced that a La France service/aerial with a 100-foot ladder had been ordered. Some of the funds for its purchase came from Civil Defence. The new truck was to have a remotely-controlled deluge nozzle, an innovation which meant that it could be moved closer to a fire without endangering a firefighter. This newest truck on strength would also be the first to establish a link with the past: a badge design dating from the earliest days of the department had been discovered, and the new aerial was to be the first piece of apparatus to wear the badge on its cab doors. The two LaFrances were joined by third in 1968. This new truck was the first pumper not equipped with hard suction hoses. Instead, additional equipment compartments filled the same space on the vehicle.

By the mid-1960s the department was getting increasingly involved in responding to ambulance — first aid, inhalator and resuscitator — calls. New manual resuscitators were added to the first-line fire department units and inhalator crews were trained to employ external cardiac massage. A G.M.C. ambulance, essentially a "surburban," converted for ambulance use by the addition of a new door to its right side, was added to the roster on November 16, 1966. At this time the department was made responsible for the emergency treatment and then transportation of victims to hospital. Before this, ambulance service in Victoria was extremely

[24] "Report of the Fire Alarm and Communications Systems of the Victoria Fire Department for the Year 1960," *Report of the Chief of the Fire Department*, 1960.

poor, with victims usually being transported to hospital by police "Paddy wagons." These vehicles were completely lacking in proper equipment; an army type wood and canvas stretcher was the sole means of transporting accident victims. The only ambulance that the city owned was a seldom used—probably due to crewing problems—1953 Pontiac.

A member of the city council had visited Seattle in the mid-1960s and seen their Medic 1 paramedic service. The subsequent fatal heart attack of a council member seemed to make such a service, or as near as was economically feasible, a desirability in Victoria. It was decided that the Victoria Fire Department, like the Seattle Fire Department, would also operate an ambulance though on a considerably reduced scale. With the purchase and introduction into service of the G.M.C., a junior firefighter was assigned to drive it. Over the course of 1966-67, the ambulance responded to 508 incidents, proof that it was badly needed.[25] A change in policy saw the vehicle handed over to Garden City Ambulances when that company was hired to provide ambulance service for the city. Subsequently, the Provincial Ambulance Service has taken over. The increase in the number of calls to the ambulance service has by the mid-1980s meant that firefighters, who are often the first to respond to an accident with injuries, have again become "first responders" for first aid, treating victims on site until an ambulance arrives. For a short time oxygen equipment was carried on an International station wagon which joined the department in 1965. The introduction first of a department ambulance and subsequently the creation of the provincial ambulance service, made the retention of an inhalator unit unnecessary. The equipment is still carried in command vehicles, however.

With the converted 1931 LaFrance at the end of its service life by the mid-1960s, a new three-ton International chassis was purchased in 1965 to serve as a chemical truck and to carry rescue gear. The body was built in the city shops and equipped by the department, much of the equipment coming from the 1931 LaFrance. Unfortunately, the vehicle was damaged beyond economical repair in a collision in 1977.

The mechanical section of the department is obviously extremely important because the apparatus must always be maintained in first-class operating condition. But beyond this, a constant process of upgrading and conversion of apparatus is an important part of their duties. The 1938 Seagrave aerial for example, was by the early 1970s nearing the end of its useful life and was in fact overdue for replacement. Normally a vehicle is taken out of first-line service after 20 years and then placed in reserve for an additional five years. However, in the case of the aerial, it was decided that the tractor, which was past the normal retirement age, would be replaced while the trailer and ladder which were still serviceable would be retained. A standard commercial International tractor was purchased and the trailer was upgraded in the department's shops by the addition of new compartments and equipment. By doing this, the department was able to keep the now elderly 85-foot aerial in service for an additional six years.

In 1977, with the Chemical apparatus having been damaged beyond economical repair and the 1938 aerial trailer at last having reached the end of its useful life, the decision was made to convert the International

[25] "First Aid, Inhalator, Resuscitator, and Emergency Vehicle Response," *Report of the Chief of the Fire Department*, 1967, p. 4.

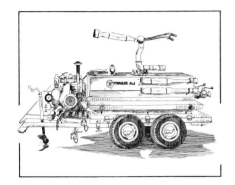

tractor into a new Chemical/Rescue unit. The basic vehicle was still in good condition with several years of life left. The "fifth" wheel was removed and a specially-designed and built body added. Chemical and rescue gear, which had temporarily been placed on a Kenworth pumper, was transferred to the new truck. Air bags to raise heavy objects and the Hurst Rescue System—the "jaws of life"—formed some of the equipment placed on the new apparatus. In keeping with department policy the rescue truck was converted to diesel. A used Caterpillar engine was available as well.

In 1973, the British Columbia Petroleum Association entered into an agreement with the City of Victoria to provide a trailer with a proportioning foam system. It was recognized that something special was needed to deal with fires of storage tanks, wharves, service stations, or tanker trucks, all of which could involve flammable liquids. The Big Brother trailer was equipped with a proportioning foam system capable of producing very high volumes of foam quickly and it was to be towed by the new rescue rig.

One of the improvements—some traditionalists might disagree as to whether or not it is an improvement—introduced in February 1971, was the repainting of all department apparatus into the now familiar "Coventry yellow," a move intended to make them more visible. The Coventry, Warks. fire brigade in England was well-known at this time for its experiments in apparatus colours. To determine which worked best, they simply painted individual appliances in whichever livery they were testing, easily the most spectacular of which was a bright fluorescent pink. Inevitably, the truck concerned was dubbed "the pink panther," and with equal inevitability, the multi-hued department became known as "the Rainbow Brigade." Victoria became one of the first North American departments to go to "Coventry yellow" and enquiries as to its effectiveness were soon coming in from distant points in both Canada and the United States.[26] A luminescent strip surrounding the vehicle has been added some fifteen years after the change from "traditional" red, to further increase the visibility of the apparatus. Headlights were made to flash from June 1972.

The department, especially from the 1960s, had to cope with a major addition to the types of buildings it had to protect—high-rise apartments. The obvious problem was the height involved because fires could occur beyond the reach of even a 100-foot aerial ladder. The answer was simple in the sense that there was really no alternative. Fires had to be fought from the interior of the building itself rather than from the exterior. In a case of a fire high in the structure, firefighters would have to climb many storeys often becoming fatigued even before they could deal with it. A firefighter in such circumstances must carry his equipment with him in a "high-rise pack" which includes basic tools such as rope and snake skin hose which could be used off the building's standpipes. The department does not use the hose provided in the building largely because its condition is not known.

An additional problem, an even more serious one, is coping with large numbers of people who may panic in an emergency situation. Visibility may be poor, breathing difficult, and the urgency of the situation leads to

[26] "General Comments," *Report of the Chief of the Fire Department*, 1971, p. 11.

These firefighters are headed to the roof to cut vents. By doing this, gases released by combustion can escape from the structure.   VFD

Chief Jim Bayliss.

Structure fires, such as this at the Herald Street warehouse of Macdonald's Consolidated in 1958, have often entailed committing every available man and piece of apparatus. Newspapers on the day after the fire remarked that had another blaze broken out, the city would have been unprotected. Mutual aid agreements with other area departments ensured that such would not be the case.   VFD

Dedicated in December 1912, the Church of St. John the Divine was completely gutted by fire 48 years later in December 1960. There was concern that the spire might have been weakened by the intense heat and so traffic was rerouted from that section of Quadra Street. It was soon determined that there was no problem despite the noticeable eastward tilt of the spire.   VFD

Looking south on Quadra Street.   VFD

The aerial had to stand some distance away in order to achieve better coverage. The heat was so intense that it was inadvisable to get too close. There are miles of hose for the next shift to gather up, clean, and dry.

STRICKLAND PHOTOS, VFD

There was little remaining after the fire, apart from the brick and concrete exterior and charred, soaked furnishings.

The south side of the church with rafters exposed.

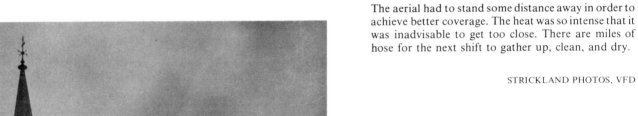

Fire apparatus is often called upon to respond to serious traffic accidents, especially if it is necessary to wash away spilled gasoline. In this instance, decapitating the hydrant accomplished the same result. Downed power lines can also be a serious problem.

PHOTOS, VFD

With closely-packed wooden frame housing—a common situation in Victoria—fire can jump from one building to the next. If conditions are right, all it takes is a high enough temperature to start a new fire. Some of the firefighters are venting the primary fire, while others are hosing down the secondary.

A new LaFrance pumper was taken on strength in October 1962. The truck in 1987 has been assigned to hose wagon/ equipment carrier duties. The 1986 Anderson-Mack has taken its place.

On October 25, 1964, the stands of the Royal Athletic park were destroyed by fire. The fire was fought from two sides.

STRICKLAND PHOTO, VFD

Close-up view.

STRICKLAND PHOTO, VFD

For once the dense smoke was not coming
from a mill.

The scene near the end of this dramatic fire.

A new G.M.C. ambulance was taken onto the roster in the late 1960s, tangible recognition of the need for improved ambulance service in the city. Before long, however, the vehicle was turned over to Garden City Ambulance and the service was run by contract until the creation of a provincial ambulance service. Danny O'Connell and George Hemming were the crew in this photo.

On May 13, 1967, the Crystal Gardens Swimming Pool experienced a serious chlorine leak which ultimately sent more than 30 children, firefighters and police officers to hospital. The 1965 Deputy Chief/Inhalator vehicle responded to the Crystal.

Firefighter Ron Steele shows fatigue increased by wearing breathing apparatus while performing rescues.

STRICKLAND PHOTO, VFD

An International chassis was purchased and converted to a chemical/rescue rig in 1965. It replaced the Kenworth pumper and served until 1977 when it was wrecked.

PHOTO DAVE PARKER

Another view of the Shawnigan fire, caught by Irving Strickland from a vantage point high on the Brewery building.   STRICKLAND PHOTO, VFD

Manning the Deluge set at the Shawnigan Lumber yard fire on Government Street in 1969.   VFD

The "fire ground" can and often does appear chaotic, in this case a house fire on Esquimalt Road on a chilly day in 1969. The LaFrance aerial and a pumper are shown.

The police as always attempt to keep people at a safe distance and traffic off hose lines.

PHOTOS, DAVE PARKER

A fire broke out in a small house on North Park Street in early summer 1974. The aerial is the 1971 International with the 1938 Seagrave aerial trailer.

The 1973 Thibault combination responded to the North Park fire as Pumper No. 1.

The 1971 International tractor underwent various modifications to suit it for fire department rather than commercial use. The fenders over the rear wheels add a touch of elegance.

PHOTOS, VFD

Though purists might well scoff at the converted rig, preferring "customs," Aerial No. 1 was an effective unit.

extreme fear in most people. One person in a panic can easily spread hysteria through a crowd, creating a mass hysteria situation, hindering the efforts of firefighters and possibly resulting in needless fatalities. Fortunately, such was not the case when, on April 13, 1980, the scene was more controlled when firefighters responded to an alarm at the thirteen-storey "Princess Patricia" apartments on Esquimalt Road. A fire broke out shortly after 2 a.m., probably the worst possible time for evacuating the tenants, which is the first concern of firefighters. There had been a large number of false alarms in the building and when the fire, centred in the storage area, set the alarms off automatically, according to newspaper reports of the incident few residents paid attention. Dense smoke filled the hallways and firefighters shared their very limited air supplies with tenants making their way through the smoke. Firefighters Fred Beadle and Hans Rudewaleit had to be taken to the hospital but were released, as did Stuart Hemmings, who collapsed after returning to No. 3 Hall. An additional three or four firemen had suffered from smoke inhalation as had three tenants, but all had been treated at the scene. As Deputy Chief Fred Severson commented later, the firefighters' actions were both selfless and courageous; they put the safety of others ahead of their own.

There are seldom if ever any centralized means of communication such as public address systems within these buildings and, because of steel used in the structure itself, portable radios are of no use to firefighters. They are, in effect, on their own. Tougher building standards — the National Building Code was adopted in the 1970s — have ensured that fires occurring in individual units are often localized there and the chances of survival in a high-rise fire are very good, at least for those not immediately involved. Below ground parking garages are another potential danger connected with apartment blocks. Fire-fighting in a modern city is complicated by another factor — hazardous materials. The department encountered just such a situation in September 1973.

At about 9:45 a.m. on September 26, 1973, B.C. Hydro official Harold Roberts was summoned to the site of an underground wiring project on Oak Bay Avenue at Bank Street. The contractor's blaster, Mark Wells, had earlier detected a smell of gas and summoned Roberts. Roberts too smelled the gas, and called in a Hydro Gas emergency crew. Just as they arrived and Roberts was peering in the window of Perikles Parisis' shoe repair shop, the building disintegrated in an explosion, pieces of glass showering and cutting the Hydro official. One of the emergency crew was slightly injured. Mark Wells, who had been standing by the open trench, moved the explosives truck out of danger, thus averting a catastrophe. None of the other Hydro or construction workers was injured, but Parisis was pinned under the remains of his shattered shop.

The Fire Department was on the scene in less than three minutes and firefighters were soon at work "knocking down" the fire and rescuing Parisis. Even with an arm and both legs broken, and face and shoulder burns, he was very fortunate: he had been pulled out of the debris before the fire had reached him. Captain Bob Cherneff and firefighter Tom Black had been assisted by an unidentified civilian in removing the injured man, who was transported to Victoria General Hospital by ambulance.

The fire spread rapidly from the shoe repair shop, either consuming or seriously damaging a total of six buildings. The Ukranian building on one side caught fire, and then the flames progressed down the other, involving four other shops. Fortunately the flames did not continue on to a nearby service station. Had it done so, the destruction would have been much more serious than it already was.

One concern everyone had immediately after the explosion was whether or not anyone else had been injured or killed. The greatest concern was for the owner of the "Little Wonder" confectionery store, Mrs. Edith Eastwood; she, like Parisis, could well have been trapped within the wreckage. The blast in a sense was well-timed — Mrs. Eastwood, as was her habit on Wednesdays, had headed downtown shortly before the explosion to do some shopping. She normally opened her store for a short time on Wednesdays to sell candy to children before she left for town. She lost her shop, but at least she was safe.

Remarkably, no one else had been injured. At a time of day when the street should have been busy, there were no cars in the immediate vicinity nor had anyone been walking down the sidewalk in front of the shops. The gas leak, it was thought at the time, might well have come from a main damaged in the course of excavation, and the explosion may have been set off by a spark in an electric motor in the shoe repair shop.

Hotels

Hotels are a constant source of worry to firefighters, even in the case of the majority where safety precautions are observed and enforced. The problem is that there are usually large numbers of people involved in a building with a considerable number of small units. Moreover, the tenants are not familiar with the building and can become even more confused in what can be a chaotic situation at best. Victoria experienced a classic case of what might be termed the "Titanic syndrome." The Royal Olympic Hotel, situated on the one-time site of the Tiger Engine Company's Johnson at Broad street fire hall, was advertising itself in the mid-1970s as "fireproof."[27] Those who are superstitious might claim with some justification that it was tempting fate to advertise the building as fireproof, just as surely as advertising the ocean liner as being "unsinkable" had been over 60 years earlier.

At about 2 a.m., on June 21, 1975, the hotel's fire alarms began sounding. One woman awakened by the noise, looked out into the hallway to see what was happening. Finding it filled with smoke, she quickly decided that she was getting out and returned to her room to get her purse and a dressing gown. Fortunately she was able to follow some men out to a fire exit and safety. Looking behind her as she left the building on the fire escape, she saw that the hallway she had just left was now engulfed in flames. Two hours later, after the fire had been put out and the residents permitted to return to get some clothing, she went back to her room. Her door was burnt away and so was the carpet. Her slippers, which she had left beside the bed, were thoroughly charred. She and other tenants were placed in other accommodations.

Reporters Humphrey Davey and Liz Hughes interviewed a number of

[27] "Royal Olympic Hotel," Advertisement, Victoria City Directory, 1973, p. 535.

the survivors. One of those was 95-year-old Harold Dawson who had a very narrow escape. "It was terrible," he said, "I can't remember too much, everything happened so quickly." Fred Wilson, who occupied a seventh-floor room, thought at first that it was probably a false alarm, but on going into the hallway—the fire was in a second floor room—he found smoke. He immediately headed for the fire escape and encountered a man unwilling to go down the steel staircase through the smoke. In between billows when the air cleared and visibility improved somewhat, Wilson was able to coax him down to the ground. Just as he accomplished this he noticed a young man up on the roof yelling for help. The fire department, which was assisted by an aerial truck and crew from Oak Bay, got him down. One resident jumped from a third-storey window to a roof below, landing without injury.

Firefighters remember the blaze as one in which some remarkable feats were accomplished, such as two or three men lifting ladders that would normally have taken six men. Adrenaline is given as the only explanation. Tragically, there were three fatalities among the guests despite the best efforts of firefighters. In some instances, it was panic that led to fatalities according to a report of the inquest held later. It was reported too that exits had proven difficult to locate. A Mrs. Lindstrom, a guest at the hotel, testified that "the guests tried to open doors on the third floor in a search for a fire exit but made their way through the window in a broom closet and onto the roof of a building next door. They then went down an exterior fire ladder." The loss was heavy—in addition to the fatalities, almost a dozen guests were injured, and there was $250,000 damage. Other hotel fires have occurred over the years which also resulted in both fatalities and heavy damage.

A New Fire Hall

The last operational fire hall dating from the era of horse-drawn apparatus, the Burnside and Dunedin Hall, was finally replaced in 1973. While still structurally sound, little had been spent on the building since its last major upgrading in 1964. The department had since the late 1950s been attempting to have this hall replaced by a new two-bay structure in a location that would serve this highly industrialized district more effectively. Construction of the new hall at the corner of Bay and Westbourne streets, began in 1971 and was finally opened by Mayor Peter Pollen on July 4, 1973. It was intended that a pumper and the No. 2 aerial be stationed at the new hall. For the first four years it was in operation, No. 3 was served by two pumpers, one first-line and a spare. A new Thibault pumper was taken on strength and assigned to No. 1, the truck it replaced there being assigned to No. 3 as the spare. When the new Nordic Ladder/Tower arrived in 1978, it was assigned to No. 3 and the spare pump was returned to Headquarters still as a spare. The Superior and Oswego Hall that had weathered repeated attempts to close it, and it was hoped, would also soon be replaced by a new two-bay hall. There was ample justification since there had been some dramatic changes in James Bay with a considerable amount of apartment and high-rise construction creating a high population density. There was a very real need for an increased fire department presence in the district. Nothing had been done since the existing single-bay hall was built in 1950.

Other developments occurred in the 1970s. There were major changes in the alarm system in 1977 which before long resulted in the removal of street corner call boxes in Victoria—there were 155 in service including private ones—and the installation of new radio and telephone equipment in the watch room on the apparatus floor. The call boxes had really been designed for an era when widespread availability of phones was not the rule. It would have been necessary to upgrade the system because many of the boxes were obsolescent, and their presence seemed to tempt those who liked to turn in false alarms. In March 1977, a new $20,700 control panel for all watch and alarm room functions was installed at Headquarters. The system in use to this point had been to a large extent "jury-rigged" over the years in the course of upgrading and had as a consequence become somewhat cumbersome. *Times* reporter Ab Kent interviewed then Deputy Chief Mike Heppell, about the system.

The box alarm system will remain in the old alarm room with a remote monitor installed on the control panel counter downstairs so an operator can still hear bell signals and check a punched paper tape for the box alarm number.

This too, is a dated but still efficient system that survived the old [headquarters] fire hall that stood where the Centennial Fountain appropriately squirts jets of water into the air.

Without moving from his chair, the alarm room operator under the new system will be able to dispatch firefighters from the main hall, outlying halls or other departments, turn on the lights and open the big overhead doors of the apparatus room and activate red lights at nearby intersections [Also turn on lights and alarm buzzers in quarters at night].

He will also be able to talk to any other fire department, police or ambulance service or firemen using walkie-talkies at the scene of a fire, see at a glance which trucks are in service and determine which watch is on duty and who is on standby [Victoria firefighters can be recalled to duty from home if necessary].

To one side is a tape recorder to capture every conversation by phone and radio with a record of the time, and on a second backup machine in case of failure.[28]

The panel was designed by Doug Phillips of the City's Engineering Department.

One of the most spectacular fires in the city's history broke out at Ogden Point on August 8, 1977 when a 50-year-old warehouse and its contents of rolls of newsprint were destroyed. It was an instance where nothing could really have been done apart from pouring huge quantities of water on the fire. The Seaspan fire barge *Sadie II* and fireboats from both that company and the Navy responded in addition to the department's conventional apparatus. Unfortunately, the barge was by that time, through disuse, largely ineffective. The loss was $4,629,000.[29] The cause of the fire was recorded as incendiarism which simply meant that it was caused by human action. Fortunately there were no fatalities. It was to be a bad year for fires; over $5 million in losses was attributed to incendiarism.

To help cope with the growing need for fire protection, and equally the need to replace old apparatus, there had been additions to the department's roster of apparatus and equipment. The new Thibault pumper

28 "Fire! Call For Help to Touch off Space Age Alarm System," *Times*, 7 March 1977, p. 9.

29 "Property Losses," *Report of the Chief of the Fire Department*, 1977, p. 5.

When a backhoe accidentally broke a gas main, a fire broke out in the Smith, Davidson and Lecky Paper warehouse on lower Yates Street. Dense smoke curled high into the September 1975 sky as Hydro Gas crews and firefighters struggled to get the situation under control.   VFD

In August 1977, an old warehouse on the Ogden Point docks was destroyed in a spectacular fire. Seaspan and Navy fireboats, as well as the Seaspan barge "Sadie II" poured water on the blaze all night and into the next day. A huge cloud of smoke hung over the city for days.

On October 17, 1978, VFD units responded to a fire at a Broad Street building built by former volunteer fire officer Simeon Duck in the early 1890s.   VFD

Spontaneous combustion resulted in this $610,000 fire at the Capital City Shipyard on July 5, 1978. Cordage, paint and other marine stores and an elderly building made heavy losses inevitable.

IAN McKAIN PHOTO, VFD

A deluge set was used to put water on these drums to keep their temperature down. Large fuel storage tanks were uncomfortably nearby.   STRICKLAND PHOTO, VFD

On November 26, 1979 photographer John McKay caught the Nordic LTI ladder tower aerial in action on Government Street. Smitty's Pancake House at the entrance to Bastion Square suffered heavy damage due to an electrical fire. The pumper is the 1978 International.

JOHN McKAY PHOTOS, VFD

A 10:30 p.m. fire at the Drake Hotel resulted in one fatality and five injuries among the 35 guests. The December 30, 1974 fire caused $30,000 damage.

JOHN McKAY PHOTOS, VFD

Rodeway Inn. This 1979 motel fire occurred just across Douglas from the old No. 5 Hall site.

Seven businesses were destroyed in this July 12, 1980 three alarm fire on Yates at Broad. Reported at 12:57 a.m., units responded from Headquarters and No. 2 halls. Mike Heppell called in assistance from the Oak Bay Fire Department which responded with an aerial.   VFD

Imperial Building Materials on Douglas Street erupted in a huge fireball in February 1981. The heat from the burning former roller skating rink melted plastic signs and shattered store windows across the adjacent street. The ladder belongs to the Nordic LTI and the LaFrance Aerial is in the right foreground, probably receiving orders.

BILL HALKETT PHOTO, VFD

This 1968 LaFrance was still hard at work later that same morning. This pumper was the first delivered to Victoria without the hard suction hoses that would normally be mounted on this side.

PHOTO, DAVE PARKER

A deluge set is turned on a block of businesses across from the burning building.

PHOTO, VFD

The carving shed at the B.C. Provincial Museum's Thunderbird Park went up one day in the summer of 1981 when a spark from a compressor ignited some wood preservative.

PHOTOS DAVE PARKER

The 1978 International.

Light globes and large panes of glass in the main museum building were melted by the heat from the burning shed some 50 feet away.

Jacks are needed to keep the Nordic stable.

Getting the water to the fire.

mentioned earlier was taken on strength in 1973 to replace the 1949 LaFrance. It was no longer possible to purchase new LaFrance trucks, because the company had gone out of business in 1969 and the parent company in Elmira, New York, also closed its doors a few years later. In 1977 another pumper, this time an Alberta-built Superior with a transverse pump panel was acquired, the first of this pattern used by the department. This layout made it easier to monitor the operation of the pump while keeping an eye on the fire. A further addition to the roster was a new pumper on a COE comercial International "Cargo Star" chassis and cab acquired in 1978.

A good deal of standardization has taken place over the years which is more real than immediately apparent. The fact that the original manufacturer of individual pieces of apparatus differs is really not important. With one exception, the Chemical/Rescue truck, the vehicles have received the same engines and transmissions—Detroit diesels and Allison transmissions—all are being fitted with fixed deluge sets, essentially large nozzles supplied by several lines. It was always been a problem removing the portable deluge sets, because they are situated high on the body and just ahead of the hose beds, an awkward position at best. Two men are required to remove one and then to work it because it has to be held down when in operation. It was a slow process. Its power was diminished because of friction loss resulting from the water being passed through sometimes lengthy sections of hose before it reached the monitor, another term for the deluge. By installing the monitors right on to the truck itself, the friction loss was avoided and setup time was not a problem. On arrival at a fire, the apparatus could be put to work immediately using the deluge with water supplied from the booster tank. While that supply does not last long, getting water on a fire quickly is of great value. The second pumper arriving on a scene would, as a matter of course, take a hydrant to ensure a steady supply.

In some cases what are apparently changes of a minor nature, carried out for purposes of standardization, are nevertheless also important operationally. For example, Victoria trucks had 14-foot ladders mounted above the centre of the hose bed, a position where it was difficult to get at them in a hurry and so these were moved to the side. First-aid supplies were increased, as mentioned, on first-line vehicles, and an additional cabinet was added to the Chemical/Rescue. Firefighters are required to know the location of all equipment and supplies on the apparatus and these are inventoried every day. Several of the department's pumpers were fitted with hooks to tow the foam trailer.

One other feature that has been standardized is the provision of preconnected foam equipment. A new type of foam provides a thin film which penetrates better—it can surround objects rather than building up in a single location on one side. Water is supplied from the main pump and there is a proportioning system for introducing the liquid foam. This new type of foam is especially useful in situations such as car accidents where gas may have spilled. As in the case of the deluge sets, the deployment of foam is faster.

The latest piece of apparatus to join the roster is a "Hazardous Materials Unit"—a Chevy 1½ ton van which has been fitted to carry

acid suits acquired in the late 1970s and the various materials needed to deal with hazardous substances. Valuable response time can be saved by having the necessary gear on a single vehicle. Much of what is carried is used to either plug leaks or soak up spills. Command vehicles now carry binoculars so that should a tanker spring a leak, the hazardous materials symbols that must be prominently displayed by law can be read from a safe distance before any action is taken. Information manuals are carried on command vehicles and these enable the officer on the scene to identify the substance from a safe distance. The fire department is inevitably called in the event of a spill and in cases where the substance is visually unidentifiable, the provincial Ministry of Environment has people capable of doing the job.

On December 3, 1986 the Victoria Fire Department, along with other agencies, took part in what was originally to be called EXPLO 86, an exercise which was originally intended to involve a propane tank leak. Unfortunately it was not possible for propane companies to take part and the focus of the exercise was changed to an oil and gasoline spill. A Petrocan tank truck was the centrepiece. The object of the exercise was to test response time and the effectiveness of various agencies which included in addition to the fire department, paramedics, the police, representatives of the petroleum industry, the Coast Guard and both Federal and Provincial environment officials.

A command post was set up high on the opposite side of the harbour at the heliport, approximately half-a-mile to the west. From this vantage point all activity at the Store and Fisgard street location could be monitored, and cleanup efforts both ashore and on boats below the spill site, directed. A layer of foam was laid on the spill site and a containment boom deployed around the spill by boats, thus ensuring that dangerous pollutants would not drift any further. Deputy Chief Pat Graham commented on the exercise two days later.

We played it by the book; because of the supposed gasoline and diesel fuel we spread foam on the street before approaching the truck. With highly flammable material we wouldn't send firefighters into a zone of danger until we made it safe.

It took us only 11 minutes to get him [the tank truck driver] out of the truck and that's not unrealistic based on what his condition was. He was supposed to have multiple fractures and other serious injuries. Our men stabilized him and put him on a backboard. They went through the complete routine, all as quickly as humanly possible.[30]

The exercise, which was monitored by three referees: John Finnie, from the B.C. Environmental Programs, Martyn Green from the Petroleum Association, and Keith Hebron, of the Federal Government's Emergency Response and Operations agency. It was a success, but some problem areas such as communications came to the attention of those directing operations. For that type of emergency, things went very well and the department has had more valuable experience. Even with new problems being posed, basic types of apparatus still are the mainstay of equipment types operated by the department.

The latest pumper to join the roster is a Mack COE with rollup cabinet doors which take up less space than conventionally opening types and a

[30] "For an Oil Spill Scenario, It Went Great," *Times-Colonist*, 4 December 1986, p. B-1.

transverse pump panel. The truck was built and partially equipped by Anderson of Langley. Ideally a truck will have all new equipment on it such as axes, hose clamps, etc., but this becomes impractical as expenses increase. Equipment from older vehicles, when it is still of a suitable standard and condition, is simply transferred to the new vehicle. Before all this can happen, however, plans have to be made in order to get the best value for the money. This can be an involved process.

When the requirements are drawn up for a new piece of apparatus, the Chief and Deputies decide what will fulfil the department's needs. Once the basic requirements have been decided, a drawing of the truck with its features identified is posted for suggestions by members of the fire suppression division, thus allowing the people who will be using the apparatus the opportunity to suggest improvements and identify potential problems.

In the late 1940s, an Osoyoos fruit grower named Ted Thornton Trump invented what has been called the "cherry picker," an articulated hydraulic boom that, equipped with a "basket," could reach otherwise inaccessible parts of trees from almost any angle. This British Columbia invention proved to be a revolutionary development in fire-fighting as it provided a horizontal reach in excess of that available by conventional aerial ladders. It was used for the first time in combatting a fire in New Westminster, although it did not come into widespread use until the 1960s. (Chicago was the first major department to introduce this type of apparatus.)

Victoria, instead of opting for the very expensive "elevating tower" or "Snorkles" as they became more popularly known, went for a rear-mount "Ladder Tower," a Nordic/Scot LTI, when it finally became necessary to replace the upgraded Seagrave. This apparatus had one advantage of the Snorkle in that it had a basket for rescue work protected so that its deluge could be directed by a firefighter in the basket. As a safety feature it could also be operated by remote control. While it did not have the horizontal reach of the snorkle, it was somewhat faster in action. In this case specifically it had another virtue — it was less expensive and was readily available having served as a demonstrator in Ontario. It entered service at No. 3 Hall in 1978.

While apparatus, halls, and equipment have changed dramatically over the years, one element in this story has remained essentially constant throughout the 130 years of the department's history — the firefighter.

Chapter 6

FIREFIGHTERS: PROTECTING VICTORIA

By far the fairest, most realistic way of portraying what the job is like from the firefighters' standpoint, is to permit them to describe it themselves. As with any job that involves danger and requires a broad range of skills, the selection process is important. There are basic requirements that must be fulfilled, and as present Victoria Fire Chief Mike Heppell describes, the means of determining how an applicant will fit the standards has changed over recent years.

I think that we have identified the entry standards just a little more clearly now, and the selection process is more clearly defined as well. We submit any applicants to a series of evaluation tests: on mechanical aptitude, general knowledge, English grammar, and physical endurance and stamina. This is done at the Y.M.C.A. under their supervision. When I came on the department [in the early 1960s] they looked for the same qualities, but they were assessed in a little different way—a man's strength was judged on his stature and the grip of his hand shake. If the fellow appeared to be calm under the stress of an interview, he would likely be able to cope with the stress of fire-fighting. We can also tell from his outside activities how he'd fit into the social structure of the department.

What the department expects of the firefighter has changed over the years as well.

Maybe the ability to go into a burning building without a breathing apparatus and to hold your breath for a long time was at one time considered a measure of a strong firefighter. Now we're saying replace that brute strength and ability to hold your breath for long periods with a little more common sense. [A firefighter] should make use of the technology that has been developed and start using his head more. The firefighter today is faced with many more complicated conditions such as processes in industry like toxic chemicals.

Though the process of training as a firefighter continues throughout his career, in no small measure as experience on the job, there is an initial period where the basics are taught and the new firefighter is once again observed to see if he can do the job and fit in. Two firefighters who have been on the job from the mid-1970s, Brian and Frank, along with Mike Heppell, describe their experience.

BRIAN: For the first three months you come in every day, five days a week over and above your regular shift. You come in for drills. You take the whole morning and you go through firefighting evolutions on the drill square with officers in charge of the shift and the training officer if we have one. That includes evolutions with hose streams and ladder work, how to take hydrants—elementary things to start with—taking people from vehicles, from wrecks, basically everything that senior firefighters do, the new people are taught. It's a question of education and they start with the very elementary things, and as time goes on, they progress into being able to handle the more sophisticated pieces of equipment.

There's no period of sitting back and waiting, you just go! You'd probably hang around the truck, help make sure the hose is all laid out, help out with the ladders—things like that. You wouldn't be expected to go into the building. But once you've been on shift a short time, it depends on the shift, it's a little different. You hang onto the back of a senior man, you grab onto his belt, and if you're going into the fire you never leave him.

Mike Heppell went through the same process in the 1960s and found that the senior firefighters and officers were very helpful.

MIKE: Everyone is very helpful, they look upon the rookie as a sort of unfortunate soul who not only gets stuck with all the joe jobs but he is awkward. Perhaps I'm painting a wrong picture. The officers in many cases—they're like foremen or supervisors—are like good friends. They spend an awful lot of time with you.

The first time on the job is without exception, a memorable experience for a firefighter.

MIKE: You'd come to work and you'd line up at the commencement of each shift: the officer, either a lieutenant or a captain would give you your assignment. He might assign you to No. 1 pump if you were at Headquarters, or the service truck or the alarm room. In those days we used to run an inhalator so he would identify those who'd be assigned to respond with the resuscitation equipment.

I was just told to go on No. 1 pump and so that's where I went. It was nightshift and it was a quiet night except that about six in the morning we responded to a truck fire. It was actually my first alarm. There was very little to it, the brakes of the truck seized up and overheated. My feeling this first time out was really one of bewilderment. I'd spent a horrified night not knowing what was happening. There was very little introductory training: I was given my protective clothing and told where to go and what to do so far as answering the alarm. If the bell hit—"Report to your apparatus and do what the officer tells you!" If the officer wasn't around, then all of a sudden you became very, very concerned about what to do.

Both Brian and Frank found that they had similar reactions to their first day "on the floor"—actually doing the job.

FRANK: The first day it was "stay with the senior man." We didn't have time to stand around because we were short of bodies and so it was a question of just getting right into the fire. I believe the first one I had was an apartment fire and I was with a senior firefighter at the time who is extremely good. I felt very confident under his wing. We had to put on self-contained breathing apparatus and enter the apartment. I got the nozzle, which was quite an exciting thing for the first time. He was behind me, talking to me as we went through—obviously he felt it was quite safe or he wouldn't have had me there but I didn't know that. I had this rush of adrenaline or fear or whatever title you want to give it, but it was quite an experience.

The fire department is a very close knit family and it takes a while to fit in and be accepted by the members. In fact, if I've spent the last two years working on one shift and have never really dealt with the people on another shift at fires, they don't know me and don't know whether—I don't want to use the word "trust"—but they don't know how far I'll go and how my reactions will be under different circumstances. So they're wanting to get the feel of you before they put you in a situation where they have to depend on you for their lives.

There is a time element before the guys are comfortable. In my case, I spent some time in the inspection branch before I came on the floor and so they had an idea of who I was. It wasn't a case of some kid just coming in off the street. They didn't know if I would jack rabbit or run the first time I saw, or got, myself into a situation I was not too sure about.

BRIAN: I'm the same as Frank, after my two day shifts — my first night on the job — we had a house fire and I ended up "taking the hydrant." . . . When I got up to the truck the officer said "Well, hang onto the senior man and away you go." We were doing some searching upstairs for anybody that might have been trapped up there. I know exactly what went through my mind as I went up the staircase hanging onto this guy. I couldn't see my hand and I had it pressed up against the plastic of the mask. I thought "This is crazy! What the hell am I doing here!" and I could feel the heat and I was all sweaty. I thought "This is just nutty!" We got upstairs and busted a few windows, and finally the smoke started to clear. We came out and felt pretty good.

From the completion of the basic training, the firefighter is categorized according to his duties while still remaining primarily a firefighter. The process of qualifying as a first-class firefighter in Victoria is a long one.

BRIAN: There're various classifications: you have a firefighter/driver, or a firefighter/first aider, or just a firefighter. You don't have to be a driver or a first aid attendant. Of course, there's a firefighter/alarm operator, firefighter/inspector and then you have officers' ranks as well. It's an apprenticeship you work through until you become a fifth year firefighter, or first class. You've reached the journeyman stage.

Some things do not change no matter how long a firefighter is on the job, and one of these — stress — is very much a part of it. Even when experienced, there is still a strong reaction on the way to a fire — in part from not knowing what is coming. It is a major part of the considerable stress involved in fire-fighting.

BRIAN: I bet 90% of the times we have a good fire, I know about it as we're going to the fire. If we get a call that says there's an apartment fire, sometimes they're false alarms. I'm sitting in the truck with all my gear on and my hands are shaking and I'm nervous as hell and I'm so darned cold, then I know we've got a good fire. But it's that sitting there waiting and waiting, that three minutes it takes to get to the fire, that is almost like an eternity. Once you're there, you don't have time to think about what you're doing. The officer orders you — we're going to do this or that, get a mask on — you do just what you're told. But when you're sitting there you're thinking, "Well, I wonder what I'm going to be doing, should I put on a mask? Am I going to go up on the roof? Is there going to be anyone hurt? All that sort of stuff goes through your mind.

The danger, the possibility of fatalities or injuries have always taken a toll on the firefighter's health. Until comparatively recently, little was done to alleviate the problem of stress, each individual was left to cope as best he could. With greater understanding of the problem, steps are being taken to alleviate it.

FRANK: We're getting more aware nowadays of the stress involved in fire-fighting, we've done quite a bit of research and have had speakers in to talk to us about the damage stress does to the body. They've done subtle things, too, like changing the loud gong to a tone system which is a lot better on the nerves — your heart doesn't jump as much when you hear the tone. Actually you hear the speaker, and there's a definite click — you know there's a call coming in, and instantly after that, the tones go, but it does give you that little relaxation.

Victoria Firefighters like those elsewhere were enthusiastic participants in sports contests based on job skills. Such competitions demanded a high degree of speed, agility, and competence.

Special nozzles and playpipes were developed to cope with various types of fires such as those between walls, in cellars and chemical or electrical fires. These firefighters are training in the drill yard at the old Market Building Hall.

What the well-dressed firefighter wore in the 1920s.   VFD

PHOTOS, VFD

Sliding poles were a quick way of reaching the apparatus floor. The hanging pull cord was for opening the bay doors.

The Oak Bay Fire Department, created by former Victoria firefighter E. Clayards, boasted two Seagraves and a Dodge hose wagon in the 1940s.

Wilf "Gunner" Matthews retired on September 30, 1958 after 40 years of maintaining VFD apparatus.   VFD

A. Leason (left) and Bill Jones demonstrate standard and specialized fog and chemical nozzles in their "working clothes," c. 1950.   BILL HALKETT PHOTO, VFD

Below left:
L. Parker and A. Wickes operating a LaFrance Airfoam and Wet Water proportioner in March 1971. Each of those containers weighs 53 lbs.   VFD

Below:
Rick Mosher at the panel of a Kenworth pumper. The occasion was a "high rise drill" in September 1971.   VFD

A close-up of roof venting taken on March 24, 1978. In heavy smoke, especially if breathing apparatus is being worn, it would be possible to fall through a vent hole. The old reliable axe is still useful.
STRICKLAND PHOTO, VFD

Dense smoke and a probably cluttered basement are not inviting to firefighting. It is easy to get lost or trapped. ROBIN CLARKE PHOTO, VFD

Percy Graves joined the mechanical department in 1955. Bob McKean, Ray Barron and Bob Hamilton in their turn have kept the apparatus in operation.

This photo of a Carberry Gardens house fire in the 1940s shows the usual mass of hose and ladders. Note that the ladders, which are wooden rather than metal, have their ends painted white. This makes the extremities easier to find in poor visibility.
VFD

By the late 1940s the turnout gear had changed. The helmet was squatter and no longer sported the high shield in front.
KEN McALLISTER PHOTO, VFD

Don't move the net!

Although it is no longer used in Victoria today, firefighters of the 1950s were still being taught how to use the jumping net. Serious injuries could result to either the jumper or those on the ground if something went wrong. This is how it would look if it was your turn to jump.

KEN McALLISTER PHOTO, VFD

Highrise drill with Brent Atkins, Bill Jones and Fred Beadle. Portable radios increased safety and efficiency.   VFD

The stress felt at night is particularly acute, and this combined with the need to perform physically without any preparation—it is like going from full stop to full out—can be very difficult.

FRANK: [Having the bell go at night] was a terrifying experience if it hit at 3:00 in the morning—the big gongs—[there was] no warning, no preparation. The system we have now is superior. We have the lights go on first so that that usually jogs you and if you hear that little click, and then the tone comes, you get a few seconds of "psyche time." There is nothing worse physically than to go from cold into something completely physical. If you don't have that time and you're doing things cold, that's when injuries are going to occur.

BRIAN: We have the time where we're on the truck responding to a fire, but you don't have the time to warm up large muscle groups. There's a better chance of being injured in our trade than let's say in the case of a person who's doing eight hours of manual labour. They know what they're going to be doing—eight hours of digging ditches or whatever—whereas in our case, it's full out and the job has to be done. You don't worry about the fact that six guys are needed to lift the ladder normally, and that there may be only two of you. If there is something to be lifted, you just lift it and often you can't think of your back or anything else.

Drivers especially must function both quickly and efficiently whether during the day or at night, both to get to the fire as quickly as possible and to do so safely.

BRIAN: The driver and the officer, within thirty seconds, have to start making some decisions. There is however more talk now before we leave because of the fact that you may have trucks running in different directions. There are hydrants in and out of service constantly and street closures. If you're downstairs quickly, or during the day if you're around, you take a quick glance at the map. As you hear the tones coming through, then the guy [the alarm operator] will say such and such an address—if you have no problem—you go. It takes five or six seconds to look while the other guys are getting their gear on, then the driver and officer jump on the truck.

We're allowed to go through red lights of course, but we're very careful at intersections and will often come almost to a complete stop before going through. I know with driving [on a run at night], I've hopped in the truck and pulled out and got to the fire scene and realized that I was finally waking up. You've had to perform almost instantly driving a truck and that's difficult.

It is not until the firefighter has been on the job for several years that he is considered qualified to be a driver. Mike Heppell became a relief driver after four years with the department and his first time at the wheel of a piece of apparatus, a 1931 LaFrance, was an experience.

Well, it was a real adventure, I can still recall the excitement that I experienced in climbing onto this beautiful machine and the satisfaction I felt in hearing that monstrous engine turning over and firing up. Of course it was quite loud, the report from the exhaust was sort of guttural. It was a very quick start because of the fuel ignition system. I was a little worried about having to set the spark and the choke and all that because I'd never driven an old car, but that really wasn't a problem because the trucks were very well maintained and they started up very well.

I'd been warned that they were a little top heavy so not to go into a tight corner [too fast] and also to be careful when starting, not to pop the clutch. These trucks were chain driven and if the sprocket on the rear axle was in the reverse position after having been backed into its stall, and you popped the clutch in low gear, the slack [in the chain] would be taken up and either the chain would break or the rear axle would snap. The axles were very brittle. We were told that whenever we backed our apparatus into the stalls, we should leave them in low gear and then just ease the clutch so that it'd be ready to go.

There was an ignition switch on the dashboard with two settings—we would switch it over to the right to turn everything on, and the other, the magneto setting for cranking. We were warned to be careful when cranking in the event of a backfire you could get a broken arm. I can't remember ever having to crank.

On occasion, as if it is not enough having to cope with the stress en route to a fire, the unexpected when you have arrived can complicate things as well. Though difficult at the time, in retrospect such incidents can often be viewed as amusing.

FRANK: I can remember a fire down on Yates Street. It was [in a building that was] the Meat Market at the time, right beside the parkade. A lot of times, what happens is you get called to "smoke at a building." You get there and there're no flames and you're not sure what you've got. All of a sudden, it's a full blown fire and that's completely different—there's really not the time to prepare yourself physically and emotionally for what you're up against. We put the ladder up and went up onto the roof. While we were there, we found this intoxicated individual who had crawled over from the parkade. He was laying with his case of beer and was having a good time. When we checked the roof out, we found that floor below was on fire and vented an open space. All of a sudden, there was nowhere to go, nothing to see, and you couldn't breathe because a wind was blowing.

So here we were, trying to get off ourselves, in a state of anxiety, and this gentleman wasn't a bit concerned. He was just having a good time. Now we can ay it was funny, but at the time it was quite worrisome because we weren't too sure how we were going to get him off. Everything worked out.

As was the case earlier in the department's history, stress is released in the form of practical jokes or perhaps more frequently, as insulting humour.

FRANK: I'm one of the first-aiders on my shift, and I guess a guy starts getting a little "mother hennish" after a while. You're trying to take care of the bodies and make sure that if they're injured they're taken care of. Well, we had an incident not too long ago where one of the brothers injured his foot, or so it went. He wouldn't let me look at it: "No! No! I'll be fine!", and the rest of the guys were kidding him about being a wimp and that he'd have to take the knocks in life. Unbeknown to me, this was a setup—the whole thing was just to give me a bad time. In the end he came to me and said "Look, you've got to look at this foot because it's really bothering me, I don't want to go to the doctor. If you can tape the toes together so I can manage to get through the shift, I can maybe go to the doctor on my own time." So here I am very seriously making sure the thing isn't broken and trying to tape it together. In the end I found out that they were pulling my leg. It happened when the phone rang, the individual jumped up, ran and answered the phone where a moment ago, he couldn't even walk.

Fire department humour is such that any incident is immediately stored away and repeated—relentlessly and forever!

BRIAN: . . . there was a hell of a lot of smoke in the place and a pretty good fire. We got it knocked down and we were wandering around checking spots and doing this and that. One of the firefighters went inside a door and didn't know where he was going—he was just checking things out. The door shut and he couldn't find the door in order to get out. We didn't know where he was because we weren't really looking for him. It's not like you're counting all the time where someone is. He came flying out the glass window of the ladies' washroom. His mask was running out of air and he just ended up bashing out the window and jumping down. Now it seems quite humorous that he got lost. We're always kidding him that we'll have to put a little chain on him or a bell so we don't lose him again.

Fires inevitably vary both in the severity and difficulty of getting them "knocked down."

BRIAN: The fires that concern us as firefighters are the ones that we find extremely difficult — fires that are below ground level and fires in which human life is involved. We start getting involved in thinking about our own safety when we're below ground, but when you have people trapped, everything else goes out the window. You don't worry about yourself at all, you just get in there and do what has to be done.

My concern with fires below ground level has been where there's a tendency for the fire to come back behind you. When you commit yourself at ground level, there is usually another way out, not always but usually there's a window somewhere where, if things get really tough, you can follow your hose line out, which is the way we normally do it. But you get into a below ground fire, and you've got to be protecting your back continuously because you've got nowhere to go — you're underground. If a person is anywhere near being claustrophobic, you really notice it then.

FRANK: There's just nowhere to go, you get down into these buildings and you haven't found the fire yet. It's getting hotter and hotter and the hair in your ears is burning. You know, the adrenalin starts flowing and you're wondering if you should be there. You end up continuing on because there're two or three guys with you and they're draining themselves just to get in there. Your whole metabolism is telling you to get out of that situation, so you're having to overcome that. It's like if you went under water, your whole metabolism would force you to head back up again. When you get to a building there're people running out and you've got to turn completely 180 and head in. It's mind games.

BRIAN: You're only carrying thirty minutes of air, that's optimum, but most people won't breathe slowly when they're active. Fifteen minutes is a good use of a bottle in my opinion. So you've got fifteen minutes — that's not fifteen minutes in and fifteen minutes out, so you've got to be conscious all the time that wherever you go, you've got to come back too.

FRANK: Brian and I were at a car park fire one time, and this was below ground. That's very, very eerie because you've got this large expansive area and you don't know where you are. You can't see a foot in front of you, you just feel the heat, a lot of cars, and you know that you can get lost. There're no bearings and you've got nothing but that line you're hanging on to.

It was a car fire and it was two levels below ground. Fortunately for us, it ended up being in an area that we found quickly. We had to extend lines several times before we could get to it. If we had had to start searching beyond where we were, we would have run out of air long before we found the car.

BRIAN: Security on these apartment buildings is very tight. You often go out into a parkade and can't get back into the building. This has happened numerous times where the officers and firefighters will be looking for a fire. They will open the door, see some smoke off in the distance and go and check it out. If they don't remember to put something to prop the door or make sure it will stay open, the door will shut on them. That happened to one of our officers . . . he got trapped there, they opened the door, went in, the door shut and there was all this smoke. The only way out was through the smoke because that's where the entrance was. They couldn't get back into the building and they didn't have masks.

Apartment buildings, in part because of their height, and in part because of the number of people involved, can be just as serious a problem to firefighters as their parkades.

BRIAN: If the smoke is pouring out the cracks, and the doors are pretty tight on these new apartments, and you put your hands on the walls and they're very hot, you know that whoever's in there is probably dead anyway. Opening the door up is not solving the problem because you fill the hallways up with smoke and the smoke will kill lots of people trying to get out of their apartments.

Firefighters have to be careful when entering buildings that are served by gas mains. The department takes the precaution when there is an alarm, downtown particularly, of contacting B.C. Hydro to see if they are likely to encounter gas. In those instances where gas is present, they exercise even greater caution.

FRANK: I remember one fire . . . I can't remember the name of the apartment, but it was full of smoke and people were screaming and yelling because there were a lot of old people in the place. We went down one flight of stairs, down a second flight of stairs, and we could see flames pouring out of this room so it went out. We had this fire out in less than a minute and we were standing there for about ten seconds. I was on the nozzle, and I turned back and told the guy "Just tell the Captain that we've got it out," and just then, up it went! There was a gas main in there and it was leaking so there was enough heat left in the room that it blew the guy beside me back about ten feet and away went the fire again.

Especially downtown you can get some of the gas that just pours into buildings — it'll lift a building right off the ground. There was a backhoe doing some work out front and it pulled a gas main, broke it and ignited. The gas just poured into the building and we were there all day. One fire started in the basement and there was nothing we could do about that, absolutely nothing. We had men and all the water we could put there, but it was in a basement. There was only one way in and there were tons and tons of newspaper or paper products.

FRANK: Ninety-nine point nine times it'll be water that's used to put out a fire. It's our best vehicle until we find out what's going on. It would be nice to use foam in some instances, but it's just not practical. Water is the agent we use most of the time.

Modernization or conversion of structures can sometimes lead to a fire remaining concealed behind false ceilings or walls until it has gained too great a hold on the structure to be put out easily. Even when it is finally discovered, it creates problems for firefighters.

BRIAN: The optimum position is to know every building that you have and to know the storage area, but things change so quickly downtown . . . I mean, you can have one type of occupancy today and we can go in and know what's going to happen if we have a fire in this building. But in a month, the business can change ownership and now you have a completely different thing in there. They've changed the floor plan and you walk into what you think was a garment sales area, some place where they're selling clothes, and now you've got them storing flammable liquids. Walk in with one idea and it has totally changed, so sometimes it's better not to know because you're more cautious.

FRANK: Remember that West Coast Savings Credit Union fire on Government Street? There were so many layers of roof and then those big two by twelves as a ceiling. They were just laminated together, one after another after another. On top of that there was about a foot of air space.

This air space could act almost like a horizontal chimney for the fire, spreading it from one end of the structure to the other very quickly. Even when it is thought that the fire is out, it is often necessary to pull down parts of the structure to check. There are other serious problems facing firefighters that they did not enounter earlier such as toxic fumes from burning synthetic materials. While there is some protection from the smoke and these fumes, for other reasons it is not always feasible to take

Sean Sparks is lifted out of a World War II command post that he and a friend were trapped in while exploring. *Right*: Captain Bill Jones relaxes after rescuing the two boys. A length of sturdy rope is still useful in firefighting and rescue.

BILL HALKETT PHOTOS, VFD

It's wet, dirty and tiring work, quite unlike the "romantic" image.
STRICKLAND PHOTO, VFD

"Just what I wanted, more water!" Not infrequently gutters overflow.
VICTORIA EXPRESS PHOTO, VFD

Hoses have to be laid quickly. This fire at 2014 Douglas Street was fought by "B" Group. The Nordic LTI, based at No. 3 hall on Bay Street, is shown in action.   JOHN McKAY PHOTO, VFD

The badge of the Victoria Fire Department once again appeared on apparatus from 1965 when it was rediscovered. Dating from the colonial period, the use of the British coat of arms is quite justified.

PHOTO, DAVE PARKER

On February 16, 1983, a large section of the block which housed the David Spencer Store in 1910, burned again. Scott Air Paks had to be changed frequently. This is Fort Street.   JOHN McKAY PHOTO, VFD

Fred Beadle helps a "rookie" firefighter with his turnout gear during Fire Prevention Week at James Bay Elementary in 1981.

JOHN McKAY PHOTO, VFD

One firefighter keeps a stream on the burning roof while the other vents the roof of the upper story room.   VFD

PHOTOS, VFD

The Ormond Biscuit Factory in Vic West caught fire in 1952, news that brought great anxiety to the author who was seven at the time.

Pressure testing the new Anderson-Mack at No. 3 Hall on December 18, 1986, shortly after delivery.

PHOTO JOHN THOMPSON, VFD

Much of the routine around a modern fire hall is never seen by the public, but it is as important as the higher profile duties. Vehicles and their equipment are checked thoroughly each day.

The Chemical/Rescue rig shows little of its past as a tractor for the Aerial.

DAVE PARKER PHOTO

The Superior pumper at the Imperial Building Materials fire. The wall in behind the truck is ready to collapse. The tires on the truck are starting to melt, and the paint on the vehicle is beginning to bubble from the intense heat.

Thibault pumper and Nordic LTI at #3 Fire Station on Bay Street.

FRANK DE GRUCHY PHOTOS

Fort Street during the dramatic West Coast Savings fire of February 1983.

Grass fires are a common feature of Victoria during the dry summer months. This was on the Songhees Reservation in the 1960s.   VFD

Randy Jackson cuts a section out of the wall at MacDonald Park on April 11, 1985. This would have been a tough job by hand.
JOHN THOMPSON PHOTO, VFD

On May 31, 1979, Irving Strickland, shown here at the lectern, was made an honourary Victoria firefighter. He had been photographing the department since 1934, providing an excellent historical record. Chief Eric Simmons is sitting on the right.   JOHN McKAY PHOTO, VFD

Roy Chudleigh makes himself comfortable while keeping a stream aimed at the McCarter Mill fire. It's heavy smelly work.

Ross Cameron carries a high-rise pack up the Camosack apartment in September 1971 in a drill to test procedures.

Gibson's Bowladrome fire February 2, 1958. From left: David MacKereth, Bob Whysker, George Kulai.

The explosion and fire on Oak Bay Avenue in September 1973 resulted in frantic attempts to get the fire under control. It was uncertain whether or not there were victims trapped inside.

PHOTOS, VFD

Jim Marshall.   WILLIAM BOUCHER PHOTO, VFD

advantage of the protection. Masks and Scot bottles can create difficulties such as decreasing visibility or making things too bulky—they have to be put aside in those circumstances.

FRANK: I remember we came on the next day and went up there and you just couldn't wear a mask up on the roof. You were trying to rip the roof apart, literally ripping the roof apart and putting out the roofing material. But with a mask on you wouldn't be able to see clearly enough to see what you were doing. There were a lot of big holes around and it would have been very easy to fall through. So although it was probably not good for the health, it was just as impractical to wear a mask.

On numerous occasions up there, the wind would all of a sudden blow in one direction and there would be eight firefighters hanging over the edge of the roof coughing and spitting up—there was just no other way of getting it out. The mask isn't practical at all times but it's good where you can't see a thing and you are going by feel anyway.

The necessity to vent a fire in order to release gases that have built up can leave holes in the roof. This combined with poor visibility can on occasion, lead to injuries even when great care is taken. The weakening of the structure due to fire damage and venting also increases the element of danger, even after the fire has been put out.

Few people realize that firefighters also carry out salvage—attempting to protect belongings from damage—and the cleanup after a fire. One shift, that which is called out to a major fire, will put it out and a second, coming on later, will often be left with the cleanup.

BRIAN: People think that once the fire is out we just leave, but we spend hours and hours on cleanup and salvage. We've got all the salvage equipment; tarpaulins, axes shovels, buckets—you name it—we're pretty good janitors. We've left fires where the place is cleaner than when we've arrived. We've done the windows almost. We've had assistant chiefs in the past who were scrupulous when it came to cleaning up. Just a matter of pride.

Firefighters are very much part of the community they serve. Annual Muscular Dystrophy drives have proven to be very successful in raising funds for that cause as have others for a Burns Unit. A mobile Fire Safety House was built by Victoria firefighters with considerable support from the local business community. Towed to local schools behind a pumper, the house serves to instruct children on the safest ways to leave a burning house. This program was spearheaded by the Victoria Fire-fighters' Benefit Society. Firefighters have become increasingly aware of their history in recent years and have in 1986 especially taken consider-able effort towards restoring vintage apparatus. The 1899 Waterous steam pumper the *Charles E. Redfern* is being restored to fully operational condition. This venture has been supported by the Victoria Machinery Depot (1986) in terms of labour and financially by the British Columbia Heritage Trust and many other individual and corporate donors. Len Thomas of the Saanich Historical Artifacts Society provided expertise for redesign of the boiler, and members of the Society have been involved with the rebuilding of the wooden wheels. By late 1987 the Victoria fire-fighters will have an important artifact in their collection, one which will be the envy of many museums.

EPILOGUE

There is tremendous satisfaction in being a firefighter: the job is a vital and highly responsible one, and moreover, not one which anyone can do. Saving property and especially lives is very gratifying. However, a firefighter may, at times, experience frustration and anger. On occasions when a hose line cannot be extended as far or as quickly as one would like or when, for safety reasons, it is not possible to go further and a life is lost, a firefighter will often wonder if he has done everything possible, especially in those instances where only a short distance remained to be covered or the presence of additional manpower and equipment close at hand might have made the difference.

If a Victoria firefighter of 1860 were able to visit the city almost 130 years later in the 1980s, he would likely be astounded at both the differences and similarities to his own world. The technology at the command of his modern equivalent would be all but unknown to him, certainly in terms of its capacity and capabilities. The city itself would have changed dramatically as well. He would, with typical nineteenth-century optimism have expected it to grow in size, but he would not, however, have been able to predict the way in which it had changed. Building materials in use would not have in many instances existed in his time, and urban transportation facilities would be unrecognizeable. The existence of a full-time professional fire department would also come as a surprise. In 1860, as we have seen, the pride in doing the job with volunteers rather than "hirelings" was intense and deep-rooted.

The similarities between the two worlds, though perhaps less obvious than the differences, would soon become apparent to him as well. Water, in the 1980s seemingly available in unlimited quantities from underground mains, would still be the primary means of extinguishing fires. Many of the hand tools such as axes, pry bars, and pull down hooks would not differ. Ladders, though of metal rather than wood, would be essentially the same. The most basic elements would not have changed. The enemy — Fire — and the dedication and degree of skill necessary to combat it will have remained the same. He would be convinced that his city and its people are in good hands.

Victoria and its citizens have been very fortunate that there have been dedicated firefighters — both volunteer and professional — who have been ready and willing to protect them.

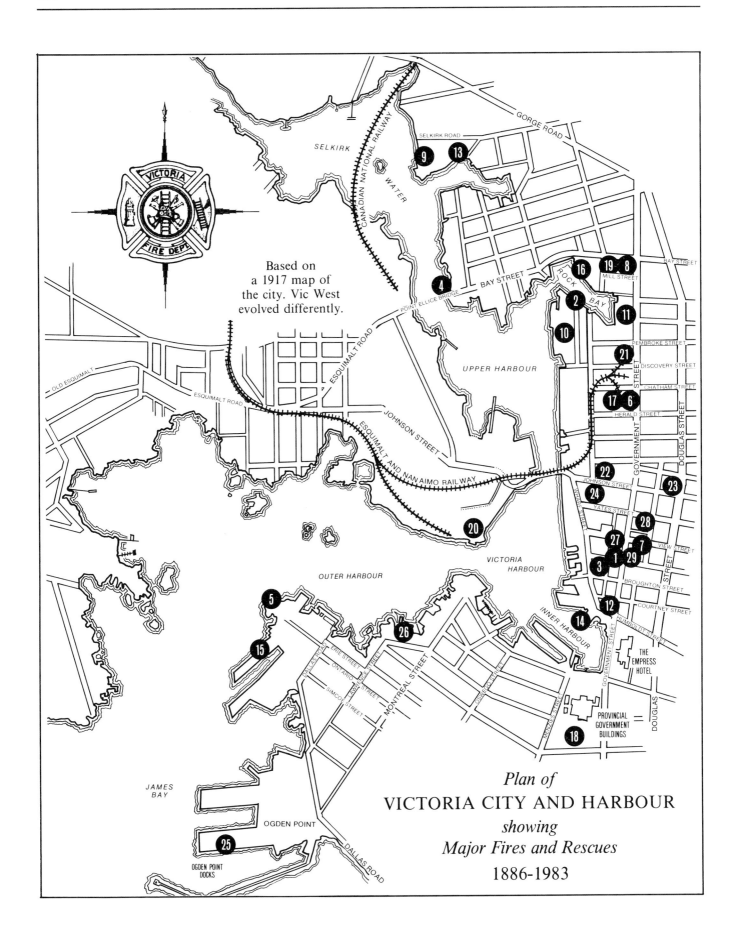

Based on
a 1917 map of
the city. Vic West
evolved differently.

Plan of
VICTORIA CITY AND HARBOUR
showing
Major Fires and Rescues
1886-1983

Key to Fires and Rescues in Map at Left

1 West side of Government between Fort and Bastion July 31, 1886.
2 National Electric Tram and Light Company August 1892.
3 Victoria Power and Light, Langley Street power house February 1895.
4 Pt. Ellice Bridge Collapse May 26, 1896.
5 Victoria Chemical Works, Shoal Point, August 16, 1898.
6 Chinatown 1907.
7 David Spencer Fire and Five Sisters Block 1910.
8 Lemon, Gonnason Company [mill] September 1912.
9 Cameron Lumber Company Ltd. [mill] 1917.
10 Canadian Puget Sound Lumber and Timber Co. Ltd. [mill] 1935.
11 Sidney Lumber Co. Ltd. 1939.
12 Post Office October 1939.
13 Selkirk [Hudson] Lumber Company 1950.

14 *Salvage King* October 19, 1953.
15 Victoria Machinery Depot Ltd. January 1954.
16 McCarter Shingle Ltd. April 1954.
17 Central Cartage Ltd. July 19, 1954.
18 Bird Cage March 1957.
19 Crowe, Gonnason February 1960.
20 Sidney Roofing and Paper Co. Ltd. 1960.
21 Shawnigan Lumber Yards Ltd. 1968.
22 Drake Hotel 1974.
23 Royal Olympic Hotel 1975.
24 Smith Davidson and Lecky 1975.
25 Ogden Point Dock 1977.
26 Capital City Shipyards 1978.
27 Smitty's Pancake House 1979.
28 Victoria Hobbies and Crafts 1980.
29 West Coast Savings 1983.

Victoria Fire Halls 1860-1987

1 Union Hook and Ladder Company 1860-70
2 Union Hook and Ladder Company VFD 1870-89 *same building moved to new location*
3 Deluge Engine Co. No. 1 1860-63
4 Tiger Engine Co. No. 2 1863-74
5 Deluge Engine Co. No. 1 1863-77
6 Deluge Engine Co. No. 1 VFD 1877-99
7 Tiger Engine Co. No. 2 1874-80
8 Tiger Engine Co. No. 2 VFD 1880-99
9 No. 1 Hall Victoria Fire Department 1899-1959
10. Salt Water Pumping Station VFD 1910
11 "Princess Louise" Volunteer Company 1884-92
12 No. 3 Hall VFD 1892-1908
13 No. 3 Hall VFD 1908-18
14 No. 5 Hall VFD 1908-73 *renumbered No. 3*
15 No. 4 Hall VFD 1899-1937 *volunteer company briefly*
16 No. 2 Hall VFD 1899-1952 *volunteer company at Central School pre-1899*
17 No. 6 Hall VFD 1911-18 *volunteer company at Oaklands earlier*
18 No. 7 Hall VFD 1911-18
19 No. 8 Hall VFD 1913-37
20 No. 4 Hall VFD 1943-50
21 No. 4 Hall VFD 1950- *renumbered to No. 2 in 1970s*
22 No. 1 Hall VFD 1959-
23 No. 3 Hall VFD 1973-

See page 220 for maps of halls numbered 11 to 23.

Fire Hall Location Sources

Fire Hall sites have been determined using City Directories, maps, plans, assessment rolls, contemporary photographs and newspaper accounts. Some of the locations identified are only approximate due to imprecise information, changing street names, street numbers and the ever changing paths taken by many streets. Some streets have disappeared altogether since the 1860s.

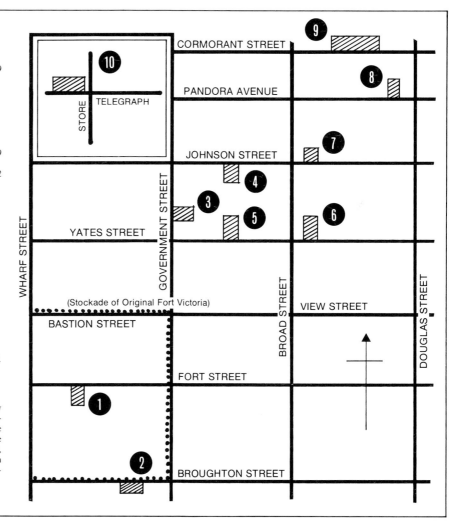

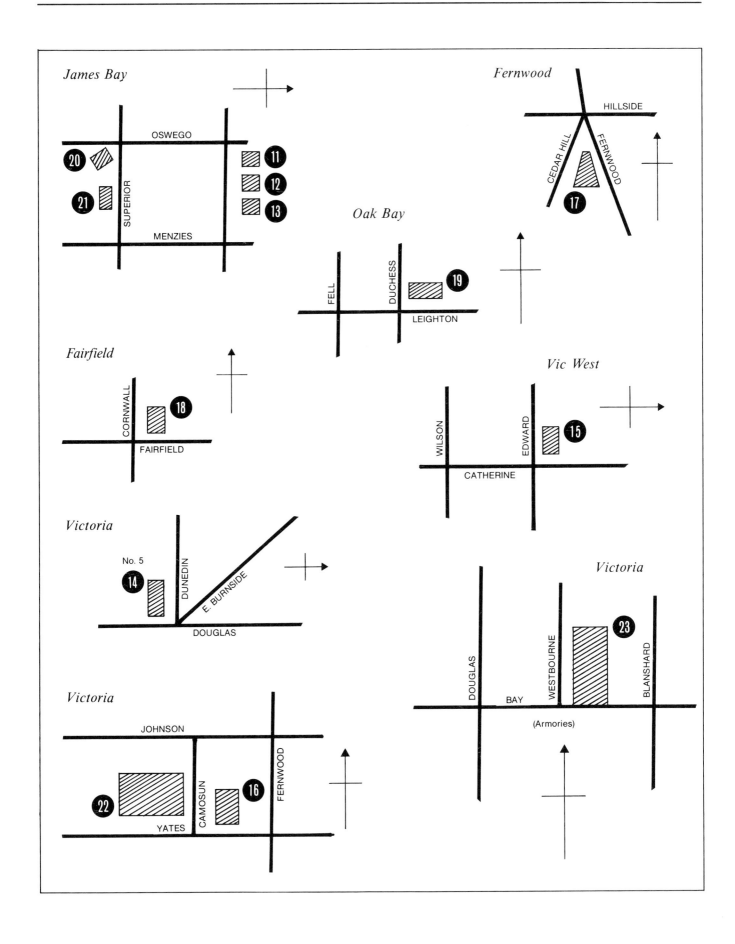

BIBLIOGRAPHY

Books

Akrigg, G. P. V. and Akrigg, Helen B. *British Columbia Chronicles 1846-1871: Gold and Colonists.* Vancouver: Discovery, 1977.

Benjamin, Park, ed. *Appleton's Cyclopedia of Applied Mechanics.* Vol. 1. New York: D. Appleton, 1893.

Boam, Henry J. comp. *British Columbia: Its History, People, Commerce, Industries and Resources.* London: Sells, 1912.

Bowsfield, Hartwell, ed. *The Fort Victoria Letters: 1846-1851.* Vol. XXXII. Winnipeg: Hudson's Bay Record Society, 1979.

Burgess-Wise, David. *Fire Engines and Firefighting.* London: Octopus, 1977.

Ditzel, Paul. *Fire Engines, Firefighters; The Men, Equipment, and Machines From the Colonial Times to the Present.* New York: Crown, 1976.

Emberson, Alfred J. *All About Victoria.* Victoria: Victoria Press and Printing, 1917.

Fawcett, Edgar. *Some Reminiscences of Old Victoria.* Toronto: William Briggs, 1912.

Goodenough, Simon. *Fire! The Story of the Fire Engine.* Secaucus: Chartwell, 1978.

Gosnell, R. E. *A History of British Columbia.* Victoria: Lewis, 1906.

Hendrickson, James E., ed. *Journals of the Colonial Legislatures of the Colonies of Vancouver Island and British Columbia: 1851-1866.* 5 Vols. Victoria: Provincial Archives of British Columbia, 1980.

Holloway, Sally. *London's Noble Fire Brigade 1833-1904.* London: Cassell, 1973.

Holtzman, Robert F. *The Romance of Firefighting.* New York: Bonanza, 1969.

Kerr, J. B. *Biographical Dictionary of Well-Known British Columbians.* Vancouver: Kerr and Begg, 1890.

Knight, Edward H. *Knight's American Mechanical Dictionary.* Vol. 1. New York: Hurd and Houghton, 1877.

Matches, Alex. *It Began with a Ronald: A Pictorial History of Vancouver's Firefighting Equipment.* Vancouver: Alex Matches, 1977.

McCall, Walter. *American Fire Engines Since 1900.* Glen Ellyn: Crestline, 1976.

Morris, John V. *Fires and Firefighters.* Boston: Little-Brown, 1955.

Morton, W. L., ed. *Shield of Achilles: Aspects of Canada in the Victorian Age.* Toronto: McClelland and Stewart, 1968.

Palmer, Bryan D. *A Culture in Conflict: Skilled Workers and Capitalism in Hamilton, Ontario: 1866-1914.* Montreal: McGill-Queens University Press, 1979.

Peckham, John. *Fighting Fire with Fire.* Newfoundland, N.J.: Walter R. Haessner, 1972.

Pethick, Derek. *Victoria/the Fort.* Vancouver: Mitchell Press, 1968.

Pethick, Derek. *Summer of Promise: Victoria 1864-1914.* Victoria: Sono Nis Press, 1980.

Segger, Martin and Franklin, Douglas. *Victoria: A Primer for Regional History in Architecture*. Watkins Glen, N.Y.: The American Life Foundation and Study Institute, 1979.

Shaw, Eyre Massey. *Fire Protection*. London: C. & E. Layton, 1876.

Warren, Sam Bass. *The Urban Wilderness: A History of the American City*. New York: Harper and Row, 1972.

Whitehead, Trevor. *Fire Engines*. Princes Risborough: Shire, 1981.

Articles

Laing, F. W. and Lamb, W. K. "The Fire Companies of Old Victoria." *British Columbia Historical Quarterly*. (January 1946) vol. X No. 1, pp. 43-75.

Thesis

Walden, F. E. *The Social History of Victoria, B.C.: 1858-1871*. Vancouver: U.B.C., 1951. (unpublished)

Reports

Bulkley, Thomas. *The Victoria Water Supply: Report to the Commissioner of Lands and Works, dated October 28, 1872*. Victoria: *Daily Standard*, 1972.

The Corporation of the City of Victoria Annual Reports, 1862-1985.

Reports of the Chiefs of the Fire Department, 1860-1985.

Report of the Fire Department Branch of the Underwriters' Association of Vancouver Island, 1917.

Report of the Fire Department Branch of the Underwriters' Association of British Columbia, 1951.

Report of the Fire Department Branch of the Underwriters' Association of Canada, 1971.

Minutes

Minutes of the House of Assembly of Vancouver Island: August 12, 1856-September 25, 1858. Victoria: King's Printer, 1918.

Minutes of the Victoria City Council.

Archival Documents

Helmcken, Dr. J. S. *Reminiscences* [ADD MS. 505/A810], vol. 12.

Colonial Correspondence. Provincial Archives of British Columbia.

P.A.B.C./C.O. F1032-2 J. A. McCrae to W. A. G. Young (3 May 1861)

P.A.B.C./C.O. F494-3 J. S. Drummond to Governor Douglas (6 May 1862)

P.A.B.C./C.O. F494-4 Petition to Governor Douglas (20 May 1862)

P.A.B.C./C.O. F494-7 J. S. Drummond to W. A. G. Young (26 February 1863)

P.A.B.C./C.O. F1032-4 J. A. McCrea to W. P. Walleford (15 July 1864)

P.A.B.C./C.O. F860-4 J. C. Keenan to A. E. Kennedy (29 October 1864)

PABC/C.O. F324-24 Memorandum: W. A. G. Young to Governor (9 August 1864)

Add. Ms. 2800 Henley, David. Deluge Company No. 1.

Fire Department Documents

Constitution and Bylaws of the Union Hook and Ladder Company No. 1. Victoria, Vancouver Island, 1860.

Constitution and Bylaws of the Deluge Engine Company No. 1. Victoria, Vancouver Island, 1860.

Constitution and Bylaws of the Tiger Engine Company No. 2. Victoria, Vancouver Island, 1860.

Company Rolls: Union, Tiger and Deluge Companies.

Membership certificates

Regulations of the Victoria Fire Department. Rules and Orders of the Board of Delegates and an Act to Extend and Amend the Provisions of the Fireman's Protection Act, 1860. San Francisco: Towne and Baqcon, 1862.

Rules and Regulations of the Victoria Paid Fire Department adopted 1st March 1886. Victoria: Cohen, 1886.

Rules and Regulations: Victoria Fire Department 1918.

Fire Hall Logs.

Newspapers

The *Colonist 1858-1980: The British Colonist, Daily British Colonist, Daily British Colonist and Victoria Chronicle*, and *the Daily Colonist.*

The Victoria Weekly Gazette (1859-1860)

The Victoria Daily Standard (1870-1889)

The Victoria Daily Times (1884-1980)

The Times-Colonist (1980-)

Interviews

Brian Dallin and Frank Thoreson

Percy Graves

Chief M. E. Heppell

Hugh Lynn

Joe Norman

Gray Russell

Hunneman 1858   BRIAN McCANDLESS

APPENDIX I

Victoria Fire Department
Apparatus Roster: 1858-1987

Terminology:

TRUCK: Applied to hook-and-ladder trucks, service trucks, and, somewhat less frequently, to aerials.

ENGINE: Applied to manual, steam, gasoline, and diesel pumpers, and to chemical rigs.

COMBINATION: When two or more functions are combined on a single vehicle, as in the case of a hose/chemical, which is referred to as a double combination, or simply, as a combination. These terms apply to both horse-drawn and motorized apparatus.

PART I: 1858-1886

HUNNEMAN 2nd CLASS
MANUAL PUMPER WITH HOSE
CART
  In Service: July 29, 1858

RODGERS 3rd CLASS MANUAL
PUMPER WITH HOSE CART
  In Service: July 29, 1858

HAWORTH AND ELLIS
1st CLASS HOOK AND LADDER
TRUCK
  In Service: January 6, 1860

BUTTON 2nd CLASS MANUAL
PUMPER
  In Service: September 1862

BUNTING AND DODDS 1st
CLASS HOSE "JUMPERS" (2)
  In Service: September 1863

BUTTON AND BLAKE 2nd
CLASS STEAM PUMPER "Tiger"
  In Service: December 21, 1868

MERRYWEATHER 2nd CLASS
STEAM PUMPER "Deluge"
  In Service: April 26, 1870

PART II: 1886-1911

SUTHERLAND 2-WHEEL
LADDER ESCAPE
  In Service: 1886

PRESTON 4-WHEEL
HORSE-DRAWN HOSE CART
  In Service: July 1888

MERRYWEATHER 2nd CLASS
STEAM PUMPER
"The John Grant"
  In Service: December 13, 1889

PRESTON (HAYES TYPE)
AERIAL TRUCK
"The William Wilson"
  In Service: December 13, 1889

MORRISON (ATKINSON
PATTERN) CHEMICAL
  In Service: July 8, 1892

WATEROUS 2nd SIZE
STEAM PUMPER
"The Charles E. Redfern"
  In Service: May 5, 1899

HOLLOWAY "CHAMPION"
CHEMICAL "The P. C. McGregor"
  In Service: May 11, 1899

AMERICAN LAFRANCE
MODEL 213 COMBINATION
HOSE/CHEMICAL (2)
  In Service: April 1, 1909

SEAGRAVE COMBINATION
HOSE/CHEMICAL (2)
  In Service: October 5, 1909

WATEROUS 2nd SIZE STEAM
PUMPER "The Lewis Hall"
  In Service: October 18, 1909

SEAGRAVE SERVICE TRUCK
  In Service: November 13, 1909

BRAYSHAW HOSE WAGON
(To serve No. 1 Steam Pumper)
  In Service: December 9, 1909

SPEEDWELL CAR
(Chief)
  In Service: 1910

PART III: 1911-1945

SEAGRAVE TYPE 'C' 53HP
MOTOR HOSE WAGON
  In Service: June 2, 1911

SEAGRAVE TYPE 'C' 53HP
MOTOR COMBINATION
  In Service: June 2, 1911

SEAGRAVE 75-FOOT
"QUICK-HOIST"
HORSE-DRAWN AERIAL
  In Service: July 24, 1911

WATEROUS 3rd SIZE STEAM
PUMPERS (2)
  In Service: August 3, 1911

SEAGRAVE TYPE 'AC' 53HP
MOTOR COMBINATION
  In Service: 1912

SEAGRAVE TYPE 'AC' 53HP
MOTOR CHEMICAL
  In Service: 1912

SEAGRAVE TYPE 'D' 80HP
TRACTOR (2)
  In Service: 1912

SEAGRAVE TYPE 'D' 80HP
TRACTOR
  In Service: 1913

McLAUGHLIN 40HP CAR
(Deputy Chief)
  In Service: 1914

NOTT UNIVERSAL MOTOR
HOSE WAGON
  In Service: 1914

KISSELL KAR 60HP MOTOR
COMBINATION
  In Service: 1917

RUSSELL-KNIGHT 55HP
MOTOR COMBINATION
  In Service: 1917

RUGGLES-BICKLE SERVICE
TRUCK
  In Service: November 1922

LAFRANCE TYPE 45
COMBINATION PUMPER,
Reg. #4421
  Shipped: July 11, 1925
  In Service: August 6, 1925

LAFRANCE TYPE 145
COMBINATION PUMPER,
Reg. #6612
  Shipped: July 11, 1929
  In Service: August 1929

LAFRANCE-FOAMITE TRIPLE
COMBINATION PUMPERS (2),
Reg. #7147, #7148
  Shipped: March 17, 1931
  In Service: April 1, 1931

LAFRANCE-FOAMITE CITY
SERVICE TRUCK, Reg. #7298
  Shipped: March 23, 1931
  In Service: April 1, 1931

STUDEBAKER COMBINATION
  In Service: 1935

CHEVROLET CAR
(Chief)
  In Service: 1935

BICKLE-SEAGRAVE 85-FOOT
AERIAL
  In Service: August 1938

BICKLE-SEAGRAVE TRAILER
PUMP (2)
  In Service: 1942

PART IV: 1946-1987

CHEVROLET HOSE WAGON
(1937)
(Drill Apparatus)
  In Service: 1946

FARGO ¾-TON PICKUP TRUCK
  In Service: 1947

PONTIAC CAR
  In Service: 1947

DODGE CAR
(Chief)
  In Service: 1948

LAFRANCE 700 SERIES
TRIPLE COMBINATION
PUMPER
  Reg. #L3963
  In Service: November 1949

G.M.C. LADDER TRUCK
  In Service: 1949

FORD CAR
(Chief)
  In Service: 1950

PONTIAC CAR
(Chief)
  In Service: 1951

KENWORTH TRIPLE
COMBINATION PUMPER
  In Service: May 21, 1952

FORD CAR
(Chief)
  In Service: 1953

KENWORTH TRIPLE
COMBINATION PUMPER
  In Service: July 29, 1953

KENWORTH CITY SERVICE
LADDER TRUCK
  In Service: July 16, 1954

CHEVROLET CAR
(Chief)
  In Service: 1954

PONTIAC CAR
(Chief)
  In Service: 1955

METEOR CAR
(Chief)
  In Service: 1957

DODGE CAR
(Chief)
  In Service: 1959

LAFRANCE TRIPLE
COMBINATION PUMPER,
Reg. #626800
  In Service: October 11, 1962

RAMBLER CAR
(Chief)
  In Service: 1963

FORD GALAXY CAR
(Chief)
  In Service: 1963

LAFRANCE 100-FOOT
AERIAL/SERVICE TRUCK
  In Service: 1965

FORD FALCON CAR
(Chief)
  In Service: 1965

INTERNATIONAL
"TRAVELALL"
(Deputy Chief, Inhalator)
  In Service: 1965

INTERNATIONAL
CHEMICAL/FOAM TRUCK
  In Service: 1965

G.M.C. AMBULANCE
  In Service: 1966

FORD FALCON CAR
(Chief, Inspection Branch)
  In Service: 1967

LAFRANCE TRIPLE
COMBINATION PUMPER
  In Service: 1968

ACADIAN CAR
(Inspection Branch)
  In Service: 1968

METEOR STATION WAGON (2)
(Chief)
  In Service: 1968

FORD ¾-TON PICKUP TRUCK
(Mechanic Division)
  In Service: 1968

CHEVROLET STATION WAGON
(Deputy Chief)
  In Service: 1969

CHEVROLET VAN
(Training and Fire Prevention
Division)
  In Service: 1969

INTERNATIONAL TRACTOR
  In Service: 1971

BIG BROTHER FOAM TRAILER
  In Service: 1973

THIBAULT TRIPLE
COMBINATION PUMPER
  In Service: 1973

FORD MAVERICK CAR
(Fire Prevention Divison)
  In Service: 1976

SUPERIOR TRIPLE
COMBINATION PUMPER
  In Service: 1977

NORDIC LADDER TOWER
  In Service: 1977

FORD GRANADA CAR
(Deputy Chief)
  In Service: 1977

FORD CUSTOM 500 STATION
WAGON
(Assistant Chief, Fire Suppression
Division)
  In Service: 1977

INTERNATIONAL
CHEMICAL/RESCUE
  In Service: 1977

INTERNATIONAL CARGOSTAR
TRIPLE COMBINATION
PUMPER
  In Service: 1978

FORD LTD CAR
(Chief)
  In Service: 1978

FORD F350 PICKUP TRUCK
(Mechanic Division)
  In Service: 1978

FORD LTD 500 STATION
WAGON
(Fire Operations Commander)
  In Service: 1979

FORD FAIRMONT
STATION WAGON
(Fire Prevention Division)
  In Service: 1980

PONTIAC ACADIAN CAR
(Fire Prevention Division)
  In Service: 1980

DODGE ASPEN CAR
(Fire Prevention Division)
  In Service: 1980

PLYMOUTH CARAVELLE
STATION WAGON
(Fire Prevention Division)
  In Service: 1981

DODGE ARIES CAR
(Deputy Chief)
  In Service: 1984

DODGE VAN
(Fire Prevention Division)
  In Service: 1984

CHEVROLET HAZARDOUS
MATERIALS UNIT
  In Service: December 1986

DODGE RELIANT STATION
WAGON
(Chief)
  In Service: 1987

ANDERSON-MACK TRIPLE
COMBINATION PUMPER
  In Service: February 28, 1987

The department will be adding a
command/communications unit to
the roster in late Fall 1987. The
vehicle, a used British Columbia
ambulance, purchased with a grant
from the City of Victoria, is being
equipped with VHF/UHF radios.
These, would, in the event of a
disaster, be manned by local amateur
radio operators. According to Deputy
Graham, this unit would only be used
in the event of a disaster such as a
major fire or earthquake.

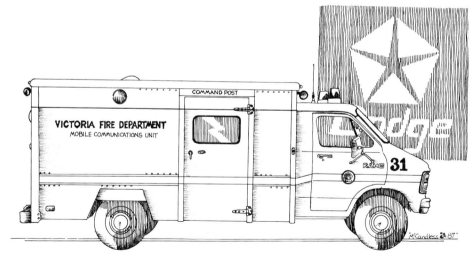

Mobile Communications Unit 1987   BRIAN McCANDLESS

The primary sources for the above roster
are "The Annual Reports of the Chief of
the Fire Department" and official "Apparatus in Service and Reserve" lists. The
former as a source varies greatly in
completeness and occasionally accuracy.

APPENDIX II

Fire apparatus has changed dramatically over the years, and one of the best ways of demonstrating this is by comparing two pieces that perform much the same function; an 1899 Waterous Steam Pumper, and a 1977 Superior Triple Combination Pumper.

Second Size Waterous Steam Pumper *"The Charles E. Redfern"*
SPECIFICATIONS

Motive Power
two horses (1899-1910),
three horses (1910)

Description (*Colonist* May 5, 1899)
The engine is what the Waterous Engine Works Co. Ltd., of Brantford, Ontario call their second size steam fire engine. The fittings are all heavily-nickled and consequently she presents a very fine appearance. She is a patent vertical engine, crane neck, double pumps, and double steam cylinders 7¾" in diameter by 9" stroke each. The size of the water cylinders is 4⅝" in diameter by 9" stroke each, having a rated capacity of U.S. 750 gallons per minute. The pumps are made of pure phospher bronze metal and the valves of the best hard rubber held in place by brass springs. There are three discharge gates from the main pumps arranged to attach standard two and a half inch hose. There are two boiler-fed pumps with a relief valve attached so that the pumps may be operated when the gate valves are closed. The boiler is 34" in diameter and 63" high with double head and radial tubes. The patent on the boiler covers the device whereby the top ends of the smoke tubes are constantly submerged in water when the boiler is in operation, thus preventing their being overheating [sic]. The best homogenous steel of 60,000 pounds tensile strength was used in the construction of the boiler and it is double rivetted, well-stayed and of ample strength, according to the guarantee, to withstand double the pressure ever required for fire duty. Composition copper is the material of which the vertical tubes are made. Before being jacketed the boiler was coated with a heavy coating of asbestos, which prevents undue radiation when being operated in cold weather. It is handsomely finished with Russian iron lagging, with heavy spun bands and a nickle dome matching the other fittings. The wheels and the truck are made of the very strongest material and the engine is a complete outfit of tools and fittings. The weight is 8,400 pounds and the price laid down in Victoria and ready for service is $4,950.

Notes
The Test was a most successful one: She was taken to the emergency cistern at the corner of Government and Johnson Streets and the fire under the boiler lighted. Then she was taken around several blocks, just as though a fire had occurred, and back to the cistern, where the connections were made. The fires were lighted at 3:04 and at 3:10 there was 15 pounds of steam; at 3:11, 25 pounds; at 3:12, 40 pounds; at 9 minutes 60; at 10 minutes 80; and at 10½ minutes 100 pounds. Two streams of water were thrown 180 feet each and one by itself 201 feet.

In reserve 1911. Preserved and under restoration 1986/87.

A steam pumper required other apparatus to make it operational: a hose wagon or double combination to supply it with hose (except for lengths of hard suction which were mounted on each side of the boiler), and a wagon to keep the boiler supplied with coal. Equipment such as prybars etc. would have been carried on a Service Truck.

The modern pumper is vastly different in that while it is first and foremost a pumper like its steam equivalent, it carries its own hose and nozzles and it provides its own motive power. It also carries a wide variety of equipment, much of which did not exist in the 1890s and a sizeable variety of tools and equipment. A modern pumper would be the equivalent of up to four separate pieces of apparatus in 1899 as can be seen from this equipment list for Unit No. 21 in 1986.

Vehicle No. 21—Equipment Check List:

Colour Code
Blue

Year and Make
1977 Superior
Triple Combination Pumper

Type and Size of Pump
Two Stage Hale Pump
1250 IGPM

Booster Tank Size
500 Imperial Gallons

Extinguisher Serial Numbers
2½ Gallon Pressurized Water
Amerex Serial No. V530748

15 lb. C02 General Detroit
Serial No. ST15-55113

20 lb. Dry Chemical Flag
Serial No. A430099

Electronic Equipment in Cab
1 Motorola Portable Radio
1 Motorola Charger
1 Motorola Radio
1 Motorola Radio Extension Unit
  on Pump Panel
1 Rad-o-lite Transmitter
1 Manual Siren
1 Electronic Siren, Smith and
  Wesson
1 Opticom II

Date Amended: October 10th, 1985.

Cab
1 Radar Type Handlamp
1 Metal Box Index of High Rises
  and Nursing Homes
1 Clipboard with Various Forms
1 Apparatus Check List
1 Pre-Fire Plan Book
1 Book Index of Streets and
  Hydrants
1 High Intensity Spotlight
3 Noise Suppressor Headsets
2 B.C. No. 2 First Aid Kits
  (under seat)
1 Laerdal Resuscitator Case c/w,
  1 Resuscitator Unit
  3 Face Pieces
  4 Air Ways
  1 Reservoir Bag

Keys: (Glove Compartment)
No. 2 Fire Station
No. 3 Fire Station
Key Vault Key (0518-004)
Alarm Box Key (Edwards)

Glove Compartment
1 Emergency Book (Canutec)
2 Pair Safety Goggles
2 Traffic Equipped Flashlights
1 Spare Chain for Chainsaw

Cab Canopy
3 Radar Type Handlamps
1 Circle D Floodlight 500 Watt
2 Pair Ear Protection Headsets

1 Akron 4-Inlet Deluge Set
1 Akron Master Stream Turbo-
  matic Nozzle 350-1000 USGPM
2 Pair Rubber Linesman Gloves
  c/w Leather Covers in Nylon
  Containers—(Behind Jump Seat)

Top Open Compartment
1 Booster Reel c/w 200 ft. 1"
  Booster Hose c/w 1
  Elkhart 1" 30 USGPM Booster
  Nozzle
2 Booster Spanners
4 Traffic Cones
2 Shovels
1 Chimney Hook
1 Squeegee
1 Ladder Wedge
1 Stihl Chainsaw
1 Gallon Container Gasoline
1 Flush Hydrant Key
1 Oxygen Therapy Unit c/w
  1 Face Piece
1 2½ Gallon Soot Bucket

Transverse 1½" Hose Compartments
200 ft. of 1½" Hose c/w
  1 1½" Elkhart Breakapart
  Nozzle, 40-60-90-125 USGPM
  c/w
  100 ft. of 1½" Hose under Preconnected Line (faces left)
  100 ft. of 1½" Hose under Preconnected Line (faces right)

Left Side of Pumper
1 Pickhead Axe
2 Akron Spanners in a Holder
1 6 ft. Plaster Hook
1 14 ft. Attic Ladder
1 2½" Inlet Port c.w 2½" Double
  Male

Left Compartment 1
1 Alemite Grease Gun
2 Hard Suction Wrenches,
  1 Male and 1 Female
1 Compothane Mallet
1 6" Soft suction
1 30 ft. Suction Rope
  Assortment of Rubber Washers
1 Pair Wire Cutters (non-electric)
1 Pair Bolt Cutters
1 Length 2½" Filler Hose
2 Grating Hooks
1 Soot Shovel
1 Gallon Engine Oil

1 Oil Can
1 Tool Box c/w.
  1 Stapler and Box of Staples
  1 Stanley Retractable Knife
  1 Pair Vise Grips
  1 8" Crescent Wrench
  1 Pair Side Cutters
  1 Traffic Chalk
  1 Screwdriver
  1 Uni Screwdriver
  1 Set of Allen Wrenches
  1 Claw Hammer
  1 Set Seat Belt Snips
  1 Pair Battery Pliers
  1 Wooden Sprinkler Shut-off
  1 Combination Wrench and
    Screwdriver for Chainsaw
2 Explosion Proof Handlamps

Left Compartment 2
3 Stacked Deluge Tips 1¾", 1½",
  1⅜"
1 Deluge Set Discharge Tubes
1 2½" S.S. Nozzle 1" Tip Leader
  Line Equipped
1 2½" S.S. Nozzle 1⅛" Tip Leader
  Line Equipped
1 2½" Imperial Fog Nozzle, 120-
  240 USGPM
2 2½" Double Male
2 2½" Double Female
1 2½" x 1½" x 1½" Akron Gated
  Wye
2 3" x 2½" Reducing Adaptors
2 2½" x 3" Increasing Adaptors
1 1½" Piercing Applicator
1 1½" Akron Air Foam Eductor
  60 USGPM
1 1½" Akron Air Foam Nozzle
  60 USGPM
1 1½" Akron Imperial PDQ Nozzle
  60-95 USGPM
2 1½" Akron Turbojet Breakapart
  Nozzles 30-60-95 USGPM
1 1½" Akron Revolving Cellar
  Nozzle
1 1" Elkhart Booster Nozzle

Left Compartment 3
1 2½" Hasbra In-Line Water Curtain
1 2½" McKean Type Terminal
  Water Curtain
1 2½" Wye
1 2½" Siamese
1 2½" Hydrant Gate Valve

1 5" x 2½" x 2½" Low Pressure
   Gated Wye c/w
   1 5" Spanner
   1 2½" Water Syphon

Left Compartment 4
1 Scott Air Pak (complete)
1 Ziamatic Holder
1 Spare Scott Air Bottle
1 Radar Type Handlamp

Left Compartment 5
1 Scott Air Pak (complete)
1 Ziamatic Holder
1 Spare Scott Air Bottle
1 Radar Type Handlamp

Left Compartment 6
1 Scott Air Pak (complete)
1 Ziamatic Holder
1 Spare Scott Air Bottle
1 Radar Type Handlamp

Lamp Compartment 7
1 Scott Air Pak (complete)
1 Ziamatic Holder
1 Spare Scott Air Bottle
1 Radar Type Handlamp

Right Side of Pumper
1 Pickhead Axe
2 2½" Akron Hose Spanners in
   Holder
2 Metal Hose Jumps
1 2½" x 1½" x 1½" Akron Gated
   Wye on Port No. 5
1 30 ft. Pumper Extension Ladder
1 14 ft. Roof Ladder
1 Ladder Butt Protector

Right compartment 1
2 High Rise Packs each containing,
   1 100 ft. 1½" Snakeskin Hose
   1 1½" No. SL150 Lightweight
      Plastic Nozzle
   1 2½" x 1½" Reducing Adapter
   1 2" x 1½" Reducing Adapter
   1 2½" Hose Spanner
   1 100 ft. of 1½" Snakeskin Hose
      (rolled)
2 Hose Ropes in Backpack

Right Compartment 2
1 2½" Pressure Water Extinguisher
1 15 lb. CO2 Extinguisher
1 20 lb. Dry Chemical Extinguisher

Right Compartment 3
1 Kevlar Blanket
1 Pair Kevlar Gloves
1 Electric Cord Reel with 125 ft.
   Extension Cord c/w,
   4 Hose Straps
1 5 Gallon Can of 3% Air Foam
1 Yellow Plastic Pail containing
   Plug N' Dyke
1 2½ Gallon Plastic Pail of Absorbal
1 Pair Chainsaw Leg Protectors
   Winter Only: Coal Oil, Matches,
                  Waste

Right Compartment 4
2 Brooms
1 Roll Mylar
3 Mops in Canvas Bag

Right Compartment 5
1 Tarpaulin
1 Mattress Cover

Right Compartment 6
2 Blankets in Canvas Bag

Rear Platform and Open Compartment
1 Crowbar
1 Utility Bar
2 Akron Hydrant Wrenches
2 Akron Hose Clamps
2 2½" Akron Turbojet Nozzles 120-
   150-200-250 USGPM

Rear Hose Beds
Left 1½" Preconnect Compartment
150 ft. of 1½" Hose c/w,
   1 1½" Akron Turbojet Nozzle
      30-60-95-125 USGPM
100 ft. of 1½" Hose under Preconnect
250 ft. of 1½" Hose

Left Main 2½" Hose Compartment
1000 ft. of 2½" Hose c/w
   1 2½" Double Female

Right Main 3" Hose Compartment
800 ft. of 3" Hose
1 3" x 2½" Reducing Adapter
   (Bottom Length)
1 2½" x 3" Increasing Adapter (Top
   Length)

Right 2½" Preconnent Compartment
150 ft. of 2½" Hose c/w
   1 2½" Akron Imperial Nozzle
      120-240 USGPM
100 ft. of 2½" Hose under Preconnect

Superior 1977 BRIAN McCANDLESS

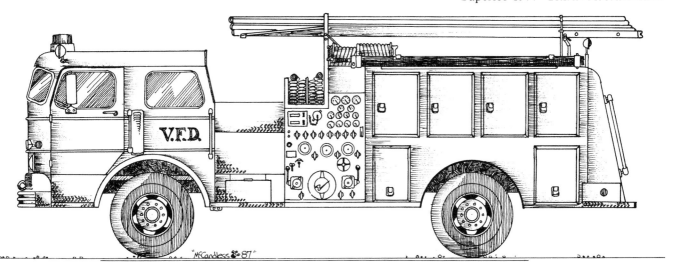

APPENDIX III

Engineers and Chiefs: 1860-1987

1860-61	James A. McCrae
1861-63	John Dickson
1863-65	John C. Keenan
1865-66	James S. Drummond
1866-67	John C. Keenan
1867-68	Samuel L. Kelly
1868-70	John Kriemler
1870-71	Simeon Duck
1871-72	Frank G. Richards, Sr.
1872-75	William Lohse

Note: 1873 was the first election for
two year terms:

1875-77	Joseph Wriglesworth
1877-79	Frank Saunders
1879-81	Charles J. Phillips
1881-83	August Borde
1883-87	Charles J. Phillips
1887-1901	Thomas Deasy
1901-09	Thomas Watson
1909-18	Thomas Davis
1918-33	Vernon Stewart
1933-45	Alex Munro
1945-49	Joseph A. Raymond
1949-51	Robert T. Brindle
1951-57	Frank W. Briers
1958-63	James E. Bayliss
1963-65	John F. Abbot
1965-66	James B. Allan
1966-80	Eric Simmons
1980-	Michael E. Heppell

On February 16, 1973 "C" Group responded to the CP Yards at Government and Discovery Streets. A man working in a refrigerator car was overcome by heater fumes.   VFD

INDEX

Service Aerial 1965   BRIAN McCANDLESS